Dannie Abse was born in 1923 in South Wales, where he went to school and began his medical training. Since he qualified as a doctor, in 1950, five volumes of his poetry have been published, the latest being *Funland and Other Poems* (1973). His autobiography, *A Poet in the Family*, a sequel to *Ash on a Young Man's Sleeve* (1954), is to be published later this year.

D. J. Enright was born in 1920. He has taught English literature in Egypt, Japan and Thailand and was Professor of English at the University of Singapore from 1960 to 1970. He was Co-editor of *Encounter* from 1970 to 1972 and is at present a director of a publishing firm. His publications include *Memoirs of a Mendicant Professor* (1969), *Shakespeare and the Students* (1970), *Man is an Onion* (1972), *Selected Poems* (1968), *Daughters of Earth* (1972) and *The Terrible Shears* (1973).

Michael Longley was born in Belfast in 1939 and educated at the Royal Belfast Academical Institution and Trinity College, Dublin, where he read Classics. He works in Belfast for the Arts Council of Northern Ireland, for whom, in 1971, he edited *Causeway*, a comprehensive survey of the arts in Ulster, and *Under the Moon: Over the Stars*, an anthology of children's verse. He has published two collections of poetry, *No Continuing City* (1969) and *An Exploded View* (1973).

*Penguin Modern Poets*

## — 26 —

DANNIE ABSE
D. J. ENRIGHT
MICHAEL LONGLEY

—

*Guest Editor:*
ANTHONY THWAITE

*Penguin Books*

Penguin Books Ltd, Harmondsworth, Middlesex, England
Penguin Books Inc., 7110 Ambassador Road, Baltimore, Maryland 21207, U.S.A.
Penguin Books Australia Ltd, Ringwood, Victoria, Australia
Penguin Books Canada Ltd, 41 Steelcase Road West, Markham, Ontario, Canada
Penguin Books (N.Z.) Ltd, 182–190 Wairau Road, Auckland 10, New Zealand

This selection first published 1975
Copyright © Penguin Books Ltd, 1975

—

Made and printed in Great Britain by
Cox & Wyman Ltd, London, Reading and Fakenham
Set in Monotype Garamond

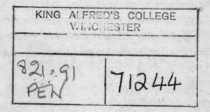

# Acknowledgements

For the poems by Dannie Abse from *Poems, Golders Green*, 1962, *A Small Desperation*, 1968, and *Funland and Other Poems*, 1973, grateful acknowledgement is made to Hutchinson & Co. (Publishers) Ltd.

For the poems by D. J. Enright grateful acknowledgement is made to Chatto & Windus Ltd.

For the poems by Michael Longley from *No Continuing City* (Poems 1963–8) grateful acknowledgement is made to Macmillan International Ltd; for the poems from *An Exploded View* (Poems 1968–72) and for *New Poems* grateful acknowledgement is made to Victor Gollancz Ltd.

# Contents

## CONTENTS

MICHAEL LONGLEY

from *No Continuing City* (Poems 1963–8)

from *An Exploded View* (Poems 1968–72)

# CONTENTS

# DANNIE ABSE

## The water diviner

Late, I have come to a parched land
doubting my gift, if gift I have,
the inspiration of water
spilt, swallowed in the sand.

To hear once more water trickle,
to stand in a stretch of silence
the divine pen twisting in the hand:
sign of depths alluvial.

Water owns no permanent shape,
brags, is most itself in chaos;
now, under the shadow of the idol,
dry mouth and dry landscape.

No rain falls with a refreshing sound
to settle tubular in a well,
elliptical in a bowl. No grape
lusciously moulds it round.

Clouds have no constant resemblance
to anything, blown by a hot wind,
flying mirages; the blue background,
light constructions of chance.

To hold back chaos I transformed
amorphous mass: clay, fire, or cloud,
so that the agèd gods might dance
and golden structures form.

I should have built, plain brick on brick,
a water tower. The sun flies on
arid wastes, barren hells too warm,
and me with a hazel stick!

Rivulets vanished in the dust
long ago, great compositions
vaporized, salt on the tongue so thick
that drinking, still I thirst.

Repeated desert, recurring drought,
sometimes hearing water trickle,
sometimes not, I, by doubting first,
believe; believing, doubt.

DANNIE ABSE

## Chalk

Chalk, calcium carbonate, should mean school –
a small, neutral stick neither cool nor hot,
its smell should evoke wooden desks slamming
when, squeaking over blackboards, it could not
decently teach us more than one plus one.

Now, no less pedagogic in ruder districts,
on iron railway bridges, where urchins fight,
an urgent scrawl names our failure – BAN THE BOMB,
or more peculiarly, KEEP BRITAIN WHITE.
Chalk, it seems, has some bleeding purposes.

In the night, secretly, they must have come,
strict, clenched men in the street, anonymous,
past closed shops and the sound of running feet
till upstairs, next morning, vacant in a bus,
we observe a once blank wall assaulted.

There's not enough chalk in the wronged world
to spell out one plus one, the perfect lies.
HANDS OFF GUATEMALA – though slogans change,
never the chalk scraping on the pitched noise
of a nerve in violence or in longing.

## Return to Cardiff

'Hometown'; well, most admit an affection for a city:
grey, tangled streets I cycled on to school, my first
    cigarette
in the back lane, and fool, my first botched love affair.
First everything. Faded torments; self-indulgent pity.

The journey to Cardiff seemed less a return than a raid
on mislaid identities. Of course the whole locus smaller:
the mile-wide Taff now a stream, the castle not as in some
    black
gothic dream, but a decent sprawl, a joker's toy façade.

Unfocused voices in the wind, associations, clues,
odds and ends, fringes caught, as when, after the doctor
    quit,
a door opened and I glimpsed the white, enormous face
of my grandfather, suddenly aghast with certain news.

Unable to define anything I can hardly speak,
and still I love the place for what I wanted it to be
as much as for what it unashamedly is
now for me, a city of strangers, alien and bleak.

Unable to communicate I'm easily betrayed,
uneasily diverted by mere sense reflections
like those anchored waterscapes that wander, alter, in the
    Taff,
hour by hour, as light slants down a different shade.

Illusory, too, that lost, dark playground after rain,
the noise of trams, gunshots in what they once called
    Tiger Bay.
Only real this smell of ripe, damp earth when the sun
    comes out,
a mixture of pungencies, half exquisite and half plain.

No sooner had I arrived than the other Cardiff had gone,
smoke in the memory, these but tinned resemblances,
where the boy I was not and the man I am not
met, hesitated, left double footsteps, then walked on.

## The shunters

The colour of grief, and thoroughly tame,
the shunters slave on silver parallels.
Propitious their proletarian numbers.
Only posh expresses sport proper names.

In the tired afternoon drizzle, their smoke
fades into industrial England.
Governed by levers, hearing clanking chains,
how can a smudge of engines run amok?

Rain drags darkness down where shunters work
the blank gloom below hoardings, dejected sheds,
below yellow squares in backs of tenements
whilst, resigned, charcoal trucks clash and jerk.

A prince is due. Like victims shunters wait
meekly – *The Red Dragon*? *The Devon Belle*?
A crash of lights. Four o'clock schoolboys gape
over the bridge, inarticulate.

Later, late, again, far their echoes rage;
hurt, plaintive whistles; hyphenated trucks;
sexual cries from funnels – all punctuate
the night, a despair beyond language.

# Tree

Grotesquely shaped, this stubbed tree craves a madman's
    eye,
its convoluted pipes lie tortured on the air,
twist black, turn back to fanged twigs and attitudes,
its dusty leaves quite stunted, still it will not die.

In rousing spring its frugal green was last to bud,
in autumn will be the first to anticipate the fall.
Now, aimlessly, I give it human attributes:
its mud-coloured bark, sick flesh; sap, a victim's blood.

As, sometimes, a child, contorting his plastic face
to make another laugh, is told to cease his play
lest abstract fate solidifies both lips and eyes,
horrifically, to one perpetual grimace;

so, perhaps, this maimed structure postured once and
    thus –
a buffoon amidst these oaks. Then laughter shook
untimely leaves down till avenging lightning struck,
petrified the attitude, a spectacle for us.

August – other trees conform, are properly dressed;
but this funny one exists for funny children,
easy to climb, easy to insult, or throw stones at,
and only urgent lovers in its shade will rest.

Yet this pauper, this caliban tree, let good men praise,
for it survives, and that's enough; more, on gala nights,
with copper beech and silver birch, it too can soar
unanchored, free, in prosperous moonlight and amaze.

## After the release of Ezra Pound

*In Jerusalem I asked*
*the ancient Hebrew poets to forgive you,*
*and what would Walt Whitman have said*
*and Thomas Jefferson?*          (Paul Potts)

In Soho's square mile of unoriginal sin
where the fraudulent neon lights haunt,
but cannot hide, the dinginess of vice,
the jeans and sweater boys spoke of Pound,
and you, Paul, repeated your question.

The chi-chi bums in Torino's laughed and
the virgins of St Martin's School of Art.
The corner spivs with their Maltese masks
loitered for the two o'clock result,
and those in the restaurants of Greek Street,
eating income tax, did not hear the laugh.

Gentle Gentile, you asked the question.
Free now (and we praise this) Pound could answer.

The strip lighting of Soho did not fuse,
no blood trickled from a certain book
down the immaculate shelves of Zwemmer's.
But the circumcised did not laugh.
The swart nudes in the backrooms put on clothes
and the doors of the French pub closed.

Pound did not hear the raw Jewish cry,
the populations committed to the dark
when he muttered through microphones
of murderers. He, not I, must answer.

Because of the structures of a beautiful poet
you ask the man who is less than beautiful,
and wait in the public neurosis of Soho,
in the liberty of loneliness for an answer.

In the beer and espresso bars they talked
of Ezra Pound, excusing the silences of an old man,
saying there is so little time between
the parquet floors of an institution
and the boredom of the final box.

Why, Paul, if that ticking distance between
was merely a journey long enough
to walk the circumference of a Belsen,
Walt Whitman would have been eloquent,
and Thomas Jefferson would have cursed.

*Spring, 1958*

## *After a departure*

Intimate god of stations,
on long, faded afternoons
before impatient trains depart,
where the aching lovers wait
and mothers embarrass sons,
discover your natural art;
delicately articulate
an elegy of the heart
for horizons appropriate,
or dialogues for the stage
and the opening of an eye.

Love invents the sadness of
tolerable departures.
So bless every fumbling kiss
when eyes, hands, lips, betray
shy, tentative disclosures,
conclusions that non-lovers miss.
Taxis, buses, surge away
through the grey metropolis
while mortals frown for words to say,
and their ordinary messages
approximate, therefore lie.

Those heroes who departed
spouting famous monologues
were more verbose than we.
Antony at Paddington,
bizarre in his Roman togs,
a sword clanking on his knee,

would have jabbered on and on
love epithets most happily,
well after the train had gone.
Let prosy travellers rage
long as Cleopatras sigh.

Romeo's peroration
for Juliet at Waterloo,
as gulps of steam arise
from the engine on its bit,
and from station-masters too,
would bring tears to the eyes.
Sooty god of stations permit
your express to dally, revise
timetables, dull schedules if it
allows one more classic page
or a Juliet to cry.

Today, I, your professional
pleb of words who must appear
spontaneous, who knows form
to be decorative logic,
whose style is in the error,
ask forgiveness for my storm
of silence when all speech grew sick;
who, waving from the platform,
found even gesture ironic,
afraid of your beautiful coinage
'I love you' and 'Goodbye'.

## The French master

Everyone in Class II at the Grammar School
had heard of Walter Bird, known as Wazo.
They said he'd behead each dullard and fool
or, instead, carve off a tail for the fun.

Wazo's cane buzzed like a bee in the air.
Quietly, quietly, in the desks of Form III
sneaky Wazo tweaked our ears and our hair.
Walter Wazo, public enemy No. 1.

Five feet tall, he married sweet Doreen Wall,
and combmarks furrowed his vaselined hair;
his hands still fluttered ridiculously small,
his eyes the colour of a poison bottle.

Who'd think he'd falter, poor love-sick Walter
as bored he read out *Lettres de mon Moulin*?
His mouth had begun to soften and alter,
and Class IV ribbed him as only boys can.

Perhaps through kissing his wife to a moan
had alone changed the shape of his lips,
till the habit of her mouth became his own:
no more Walter Wazo, enemy No. 1.

'Boy', he'd whine, 'yes, please decline the verb to have',
in tones dulcet and mild as a girl.
'Sorry sir, can't sir, must go to the lav,'
whilst Wazo stared out of this world.

Till one day in May Wazo buzzed like a bee
and stung, twice, many a warm, inky hand;
he stormed through the form, a catastrophe,
returned to this world, No. 1.

Alas, alas, to the Vth Form's disgrace
nobody could quote Villon to that villain.
Again the nasty old mouth zipped on his face,
and not a weak-bladdered boy in the class.

Was Doreen being kissed by a Mr Anon?
Years later, I purred, 'Your dear wife, Mr Bird?' –
Teeth bared, how he *glared* before stamping on;
and suddenly I felt sorry for the bastard.

# *Odd*

In front of our house in Golders Green
the lawn, like a cliché, mutters 'Rose bushes.'
The whole suburb is very respectable.
Ugly men drive past in funeral suits,
from their necks you can tell they're overweight.

Sodium lamp-posts, at night, hose empty roads
with gold which treacles over pavement trees,
polishes brittle hedges, clings on closed, parked cars.
If a light should fly on in an upstairs room
odds on two someones are going to sleep.

It's unusual to meet a beggar,
you hardly ever see a someone drunk.
It's a nice, clean, quiet, religious place.
For my part, now and then, I want to scream:
thus, by the neighbours, am considered odd.

From the sensible wastes of Golders Green
I journey to Soho where a job owns me.
Soho is not a respectable place.
Underweight women in the gamiest of skirts
bleed a smile of false teeth at ugly men.

Later, the dark is shabby with paste electric
of peeporamas, brothels, clubs and pubs,
restaurants that sport sallow waiters who cough.
If a light should fly on in an upstairs room
odds on two someones are going to bed.

It's customary to see many beggars,
common to meet people roaring and drunk.
It's a nice, loud, dirty, irreligious place.
For my part, now and then, I want to scream:
thus, by Soho friends, am considered odd.

## *Even*

Coffee-time morning, down the gradient,
like a shop window for Jehovah,
they pass my gate to the synagogue
as Saturday skies vault over.

Dressed like that they lose their charm
who carry prayer books, wear a hat.
I don't like them, I don't like them,
and guilty fret – just thinking that.

I don't like them, I don't like them –
again the dodgy thought comes through:
could it be I am another
tormented, anti-semite Jew?

No. Next morning on the Sunday,
processions uphill, piebald, lurch,
in the opposite direction,
towards the ivy-covered church.

Look, dressed for Christ and hygiene,
they glare back like Swiss-Germans
spruced and starched in piety,
and fag on slow as sermons.

All God's robots lose their charm
who carry prayer books, wear a hat.
I don't like them, I don't like them,
and feel less guilty thinking that.

So let both ministers propound
the pathology of religions,
and pass my gate you zealots of
scrubbed, excremental visions.

## As I was saying

Yes, madam, as a poet I *do* take myself seriously,
and, since I have a young, questioning family, I suppose
I should know something about English wild flowers:
the shape of their leaves, when this and that one grows,
how old mythologies attribute strange powers
to this or that one. Urban, I should mug up anew
the pleasant names: Butterbur, Ling, and Lady's Smock,
Jack-by-the-Hedge, Cuckoo-Pint, and Feverfew,
even the Stinking Hellebore – all in that W. H. Smith book
I could bring home for myself (inscribed to my daughter)
to swot, to know which is this and which that one,
what honours the high cornfield, what the low water,
under the slow-pacing clouds and occasional sun
of England.

But no! Done for in the ignorant suburb,
I'll drink Scotch, neurotically stare through glass
at the rainy lawn, at green stuff, nameless birds,
and let my daughter, madam, go to nature class.
I'll not compete with those nature poets you advance,
some in country dialect, and some in dialogue
with the country – few as calm as their words:
Wordsworth, Barnes, sad John Clare who ate grass.

## Not Adlestrop

Not Adlestrop, no – besides, the name
hardly matters. Nor did I languish in June heat.
Simply, I stood, too early, on the empty platform,
and the wrong train came in slowly, surprised, stopped.
Directly facing me, from a window,
a very, *very* pretty girl leaned out.

When I, all instinct,
stared at her, she, all instinct, inclined her head away
as if she'd divined the much married life in me,
or as if she might spot, up platform,
some unlikely familiar.

For my part, under the clock, I continued
my scrutiny with unmitigated pleasure.
And she knew it, she certainly knew it, and would not
glance at me in the silence of not Adlestrop.

Only when the train heaved noisily, only
when it jolted, when it slid away, only *then*,
daring and secure, she smiled back at my smile,
and I, daring and secure, waved back at her waving.
And so it was, all the way down the hurrying platform
as the train gathered atrocious speed
towards Oxfordshire or Gloucestershire.

## Close up

Often you seem to be listening to a music
that others cannot hear. Rilke would have loved you:
you never intrude, you never ask questions
of those, crying in the dark, who are most near.

You always keep something of yourself to yourself
in the electric bars, even in bedrooms.
Rilke would have praised you: your nearness is far,
and, therefore, your distance like the very stars.

Yet some things you miss and some things you lose
by keeping your arm outstretched; and some things
you'll never know unless one, at least, knows you
like a close-up, in detail – blow by human blow.

# Remembering Miguel Hernandez

The noise of many knuckles on metal,
we do not hear it.
There is lightning when we are asleep
and thunder that does not speak;
there are guitars without strings
and nightingales with tongues of glass.

Yet even if we imagine it,
the metal sound of bolts shut to,
then feet stamping down echoing corridors,
what can we do who stroll on easy grass,
who smile back at the gracious and the goodlooking?

Righteous the rhetoric of indignation,
but protesting poems, like the plaster angels,
are impotent. They commit no crimes,
they pass no laws; they grant amnesty
only to those who, in safety, write them.

## *A night out*

Friends recommended the new Polish film
at the Academy in Oxford Street.
So we joined the ever melancholy queue
of cinemas. A wind blew faint suggestions
of rain towards us, and an accordion.
Later, uneasy, in the velvet dark
we peered through the cut-out, oblong window
at the spotlit drama of our nightmares:
images of Auschwitz almost authentic,
the human obscenity in close-up.
Certainly we could imagine the stench.

Resenting it, we forgot the barbed wire
was but a prop, and could not scratch an eye:
those striped victims merely actors, like us.
We saw the Camp orchestra assembled,
we heard the solemn gaiety of Bach,
scored by the loud arrival of an engine,
its impotent cry, and its guttural trucks.
We watched, as we munched milk chocolate,
trustful children, no older than our own,
strolling into the chambers without fuss,
whilst smoke, black and curly, oozed from chimneys.

Afterwards, at a loss, we sipped coffee
in a bored espresso bar near by
saying very little. You took off one glove.
Then to the comfortable suburb swiftly
where, arriving home, we garaged the car.
We asked the au pair girl from Germany

if anyone had phoned at all, or called,
and, of course, if the children had woken.
Reassured, together we climbed the stairs,
undressed together, and naked together,
in the dark, in the marital bed, made love.

## Hunt the thimble

Hush now. You cannot describe it.

Is it like heavy rain falling,
and lights going on, across the fields,
in the new housing estate?

Cold, cold. Too domestic, too
temperate, too devoid of history.

Is it like a dark windowed street at night,
the houses uncurtained, the street deserted?

Colder. You are getting colder,
and too romantic, too dream-like.
You cannot describe it.

The brooding darkness then,
that breeds inside a cathedral
of a provincial town in Spain?

In Spain, also, but not Spanish.
In England, if you like, but not English.
It remains, even when obscure, perpetually.
Aged, but ageless, you cannot describe it.
No, you are cold, altogether too cold.

Aha – the blue sky over Ampourias,
the blue sky over Lancashire for that matter . . .

You cannot describe it.

... obscured by clouds?
*I must know what you mean.*

Hush, hush.

Like those old men in hospital dying,
who, unaware strangers stand around their bed,
stare obscurely, for a long moment,
at one of their own hands raised –
which perhaps is bigger than the moon again –
and then, drowsy, wandering, shout out, 'Mama'.

Is it like that? Or hours after that even:
the darkness inside a dead man's mouth?

No, no, I have told you:
you are cold, and you cannot describe it.

## *Pathology of colours*

I know the colour rose, and it is lovely,
but not when it ripens in a tumour;
and healing greens, leaves and grass, so springlike,
in limbs that fester are not springlike.

I have seen red-blue tinged with hirsute mauve
in the plum-skin face of a suicide.
I have seen white, china white almost, stare
from behind the smashed windscreen of a car.

And the criminal, multi-coloured flash
of an H-bomb is no more beautiful
than an autopsy when the belly's opened –
to show cathedral windows never opened.

So in the simple blessing of a rainbow,
in the bevelled edge of a sunlit mirror,
I have seen, visible, Death's artifact
like a soldier's ribbon on a tunic tacked.

## In Llandough Hospital

'To hasten night would be humane,'
I, a doctor, beg a doctor,
for still the darkness will not come –
his sunset slow, his first star pain.

I plead: 'We know another law.
For one maimed bird we'd do as much,
and if a creature need not suffer
must he, for etiquette, endure?'

Earlier, 'Go now, son,' my father said,
for my sake commanding me.
Now, since death makes victims of us all,
he's thin as Auschwitz in that bed.

Still his courage startles me. The fears
I'd have, he has none. Who'd save
Socrates from the hemlock,
or Winkelried from the spears?

We quote or misquote in defeat,
in life, and at the camps of death.
Here comes the night with all its stars,
bright butchers' hooks for man and meat.

I grasp his hand so fine, so mild,
which still is warm surprisingly;
not a handshake either, father,
but as I used to when a child.

And as a child can't comprehend
what germinates philosophy,
so like a child I question why
night with stars, then night without end.

## Two small stones

After the therapy of the grave ritual
(even mourners who weep circumspectly weep less long)
'A fine man.' No one snarled the priest was wrong.
Relatives pressed limp hands, filed out, heads bowed,
emotional as opera singers. But mute their song.

I do not know why I picked up two small stones
(bits of broken sky trailed on the gravel path)
and dropped them in my pocket. No epitaph,
no valediction pardoned me. Why didn't I cry,
and why won't I throw these stones away? Don't laugh.

## Not beautiful

In all hiroshimas, in raw and raving voices,
  live skeletons of the Camp, flies hugging faeces,
    in war, in famine, he'd find the beautiful.

Being saintly, his vocation was to find it
  at the dying bedside, in the disrobing dead.
    And what he did, they said, you should be trying.

Well, once, while dissecting a nerve in a cadaver
  my cigarette dropped, fell into its abdomen.
    I picked it up. I puffed out the smoke of hell.

Yet still was not fit for time to come: the freehold grave,
  things run over like slush all bloody and throbbing –
    for though they were dumb, not beautiful, I said.

It's the parable again of the three wise men:
  the first who, with finger and thumb, tweaked his nostrils,
    and the second who pressed his eyes to his palms,

whilst the third, the wisest, cried, 'Oh what beautiful,
  white teeth have these vermin which died.' *Homo sum,*
    etc., but the third was divine (as they said).

One sees the good point, of course, and may admire it;
  but, sometimes, I think that to curse is more sacred
    than to pretend by affirming. And offend.

## The smile was

one thing I waited for always
after the shouting
after the palaver
the perineum stretched to pain
the parched voice of the midwife
                    Push! Push!
and I can't, and the rank
sweet smell of the gas
and
                    I can't
as she whiffed cotton wool
inside her head
as the hollow stones of gas
dragged
            her
                down
from the lights above
to the river-bed, to the real stones.
                    Push! Push!
as she floated up again
muscles tensed, to the electric
till the little head was crowned;
and I shall wait again
for the affirmation.

For it is such:
that effulgent, tender, satisfied
smile of a woman
who, for the first time,
hears the child crying the world
for the very first time.

That agreeable, radiant smile –
no man can smile it
no man can paint it
as it develops without fail,
after the gross, physical, knotted,
granular, bloody endeavour.

Such a pure spirituality, from all that!
It occupies the face
and commands it.

Out of relief
you say, reasonably thinking of the reasonable,
swinging, lightness of any reprieve,
the joy of it, almost helium in the head.

So wouldn't you?
And truly there's always the torture of the unknown.
There's always the dream of pregnant women,
blood of the monster in the blood of the child;
and we all know of generations lost
like words faded on a stone,
of minds blank or wild with genetic mud.

And couldn't you
smile like that?


Not like that, no, never,
not with such indefinable
dulcitude as that.
And so she smiles
with eyes as brown as a dog's
or eyes blue-mad as a doll's
it makes no odds
whore, beauty, or bitch,
it makes no odds
illimitable chaste happiness
in that smile

as new life-in-the-world
for the first time cries the world.
No man can smile like that.

**2**

No man can paint it.
Da Vinci sought it out
yet was far, far, hopelessly.
Leonardo, you only made
Mona Lisa look six months gone!

I remember the smile of the Indian.
I told him
              Fine, finished,
you are cured
and he sat there smiling sadly.
Any painter could paint it
the smile of a man resigned
saying
              Thank you, doctor,
You have been kind
and then, as in melodrama,
              How long
have I to live?
The Indian smiling, resigned,
all the fatalism of the East.

So one starts again, also smiling,
              All is well
you are well, you are cured.
And the Indian still smiling

his assignations with death
still shaking his head, resigned.
                    Thank you
for telling me the truth, doctor.
Two months? Three months?
And beginning again
                    and again
whatever I said, thumping the table,
however much I reassured him
the more he smiled the conspiratorial
smile of a damned, doomed man.

Now a woman, a lady, a whore,
a bitch, a beauty, whatever,
                    the child's face crumpled,
as she becomes the mother
she smiles differently, ineffably.

3

As different as
the smile of my colleague,
his eyes reveal it,
his ambiguous assignations,
good man, good surgeon,
whose smile arrives of its own accord
                    from nowhere
like flies to a dead thing
when he makes the first incision.

Who draws a line of blood
across the soft, white flesh
as if something beneath,
desiring violence, had beckoned him;

who draws a ritual wound,
a calculated wound
to heal – to heal,
but still a wound –
good man, good surgeon,
his smile as luxuriant
as the smile of Peter Lorre.

So is the smile of my colleague,
the smile of a man
secretive behind the mask.

The smile of war.

But the smile, the smile
of the new mother,
what
        an extraordinary
              open thing
                    it is.

4

Walking home tonight I saw
an ordinary occurrence
hardly worth remarking on:
an unhinged star, a streaking gas,
and I thought how lovely
destruction is when it is far.
Ruined it slid
on the dead dark towards fiction:
its lit world disappeared
phut, through one punched hole or another,
slipped unseen down the back of the sky
into another time.

Never,
not for one single death
can I forget we die with the dead,
and the world dies with us;
yet
in one, lonely,
small child's birth
all the tall dead rise
to break the crust of the imperative earth.

No wonder the mother smiles
a wonder like that,
a lady, a whore, a bitch, a beauty.
Eve smiled like that
when she heard Seth cry out Abel's dark,
earth dark, the first dark
eeling on the deep sea-bed
struggling on the real stones.
Hecuba, Cleopatra, Lucretia Borgia,
Annette Vallon smiled like that.

They all, still, smile like that,
when the child first whimpers like a seagull
the ancient smile reasserts itself
instinct with a return
so outrageous and so shameless;
the smile the smile
always the same
                an uncaging
                        a freedom.

## *Forgotten*

That old country I once said I'd visit
when older. Can no one tell me its name?
Odd, to have forgotten what it is called.
I would recognize the name if I heard it.
So many times I have searched the atlas
with a prowling convex lens – to no avail.

I know the geography of the great world
has changed; the war, the peace, the deletions
of places – red pieces gone forever,
and names of countries altered forever:
Gold Coast Ghana, Persia become Iran,
Siam Thailand, and hell now Vietnam.

People deleted. Must I sleep again to reach it,
to find the back door opening to a field,
a barking of dogs, and a path that leads back?
One night in pain, the dead middle of night,
will I awake again, know who I am,
the man from somewhere else, and the place's name?

## A new diary

This clerk-work, this first January chore
of who's in, who's out. A list to think about
when absences seem to shout, Scandal! Outrage!
So turning to the blank, prefatory page
I transfer most of the names and phone tags
from last year's diary. True, Meadway, Speedwell,
Mountview, are computer-changed into numbers,
and already their pretty names begin to fade
like Morwenna, Julie, Don't-Forget-Me-Kate,
grassy summer girls I once swore love to.
These, whispering others and time will date.

Cancelled, too, a couple someone else betrayed,
one man dying, another mind in rags.
And remembering them my clerk-work flags,
bitterly flags, for all lose, no one wins,
those in, those out, *this* at the heart of things.
So I stop, ask: whom should I commemorate,
and who, perhaps, is crossing out my name now
from some future diary? Oh my God,
Morwenna, Julie, don't forget me, Kate.

## Three street musicians

Three street musicians in mourning overcoats
worn too long, shake money boxes this morning,
then, afterwards, play their suicide notes.

The violinist in chic, black spectacles, blind,
the stout tenor with a fake Napoleon stance,
and the loony flautist following behind,

they try to importune us, the busy living,
who hear melodic snatches of music hall
above unceasing waterfalls of traffic.

Yet if anything can summon back the dead
it is the old-time sound, old obstinate tunes,
such as they achingly render and suspend:

'The Minstrel Boy', 'Roses of Picardy'.
No wonder cemeteries are full of silences
and stones keep down the dead that they defend.

Stones too light! Airs irresistible!
Even a dog listens, one paw raised, while the stout,
loud man amazes with nostalgic notes – though half boozed

and half clapped out. And, as breadcrumbs thrown
on the ground charm sparrows down from nowhere,
now, suddenly, there are too many ghosts about.

## Miss Book World

We, the judges, a literary lot,
peep-tom legitimately at these beauties,
give marks for legs and breasts, make remarks
low or pompous like most celebrities;
not that we are, but they imagine us so
who parade blatantly as camera-lights flash
crazily for a glossy page and cash.

Perhaps some girls entered for a giggle,
but all walk slave-like in this ritual fuss
of unfunny compère, funny applause,
spotlit dream-girls displayed, a harem for us;
not that they are, but we imagine them so,
with Miss Book World herself just barely flawed,
almost perfect woman, almost perfect fraud.

The illusion over, half the contestants
still fancy themselves in their knock-out pose,
while we literati return to the real
world of fancy, great poetry and prose;
not that it is, but we imagine it so,
great vacant visions in which we delight,
as if we see the stars not only at night.

DANNIE ABSE

## The death of aunt Alice

Aunt Alice's funeral was orderly,
each mourner correct, dressed in decent black,
not one balding relative berserk with an axe.
Poor Alice, where's your opera-ending?
For alive you relished high catastrophe,
your bible Page One of a newspaper.

You talked of typhoid when we sat to eat;
Fords on the M4, mangled, upside down,
just when we were going for a spin;
and, at London airport, as you waved us off,
how you fatigued us with 'metal fatigue',
vague shapes of Boeings bubbling under seas.

Such disguises and such transformations!
Even trees were but factories for coffins,
rose bushes decoys to rip boys' eyes with thorns.
Sparrows became vampires, spiders had designs,
and your friends also grew SPECTACULAR,
none to bore you by dying naturally.

A. had both kidneys removed in error
at Guy's. 'And such a clever surgeon too.'
B., one night, fell screaming down a liftshaft.
'Poor fellow, he never had a head for heights.'
C., so witty, so feminine, 'Pity
*she* ended up in a concrete-mixer.'

But now, never again, Alice, will you utter
gory admonitions as some do oaths.
Disasters that lit your eyes will no more
unless, trembling up there, pale saints listen
to details of their bloody martyrdoms,
all their tall stories, your eternity.

## Car journeys

### 1 Down the M4

Me! dutiful son going back to South Wales, this time afraid
to hear my mother's news. Too often, now, her friends
    are disrobed,
and my aunts and uncles, too, go into the hole, one by one.
The beautiful face of my mother is in its ninth decade.

Each visit she tells me the monotonous story of clocks.
'Oh dear,' I say, or 'how funny,' till I feel my hair turning
    grey
for I've heard that perishable one two hundred times before–
like the rugby 'amateurs' with golden sovereigns in their
    socks.

Then the Tawe ran fluent and trout-coloured over stones
    stonier,
more genuine; then Annabella, my mother's mother,
    spoke Welsh
with such an accent the village said, 'Tell the truth, fach,
you're no Jewess. *They're* from the Bible. *You're* from
    Patagonia!'

I'm driving down the M4 again under bridges that leap
over me then shrink in my side mirror. Ystalyfera is farther
than smoke and God further than all distance known. I
    whistle
no hymn but an old Yiddish tune my mother knows.
    It won't keep.

### 2   Incident on a summer night

The route not even in the A.A. book.
I'm nowhere, I thought, driving slowly
because of the raw surface of the lane
that developed between converging hedges;
then, soon, fabulous in the ghastly wash
of headlights, a naked man approached
crying without inhibition, one hand to his face,
his somehow familiar mouth agape.

Surely he could see me?
From the two moth-filled headlights
surely he would draw back, change his pace?
This road to Paradise, I muttered.
At last I passed him or say, rather, he passed me.
Afterwards, the accelerating lane widened
and long lights fumbled, momentarily,
hedges, hurtling gate, country wall, amazing tree.

### 3   I sit in my parked car

And they, too, seem like images from sleep:
this Asian child and shadow
playing on a rubbish heap;
that old man incognito
preaching to the pigeons.
'Kill the Reds,' he says, 'kill the Reds.'
I wind up the car window.

Nearby, sunlight on a broken bottle
throws trinket colours on a stone,
but the ancient man in smoked glasses
walks to the right alone
mouthing a forgotten language,
walks out of sight, off the page.

And I? I leave the car, feel dizzy –
even the plastic seating's hot.
Grounded pigeons purr their gutturals,
the pistons in their heads are busy.
When the door slams its small shot
the pigeons reach for the sky,
the shadow chases the child.

In Hotel Insomnia, once, at dawn,
I thought I heard those pigeons' wings
whirring outside my numbered door.
It was only the lift gone wild.
Up and down on a nightmare ride
its gates opened at each floor,
gates of ivory or of horn:
no Asian child, nor ancient man,
nobody at all inside.


### 4   *Driving home*

Opposing carbeams wash my face.
Such flickerings hypnotize. To keep awake
I listen to the B.B.C. through cracklings
of static, fade-outs under bridges,
to a cool expert who, in lower case,
computes and graphs 'the ecological
disasters that confront the human race.'

Almost immediately (ironically?),
I see blue flashing lights ahead and brake
before a car accordioned, floodlit, men heaving
at a stretcher, an ambulance oddly angled, tame, in wait.
Afterwards, silent, I drive home cautiously
where, late, the eyes of my youngest child
flicker dreamily, and are full of television.

'He's waited up,' his mother says, 'to say goodnight.'
My son smiles briefly. Such emotion! I surprise
myself and him when I hug him tight.

## Miracles

Last night, the priest dreamed he quit his church
at midnight, and then saw vividly
a rainbow in the black sky.
I said, every day, you can see
conjunctions equally odd – awake and sane, that is –
a tangerine on the snow, say.
Such things are no more incredible than God.

Such things, said the priest, do not destroy a man,
but seeing a rainbow in the night sky
– awake and sane, that is – why, doctor,
like a gunshot that could destroy a man.
That would not allow him to believe in anything,
neither to praise nor blame. A doctor must believe
in miracles but I, a priest, dare not.

Then my incurable cancer patient,
the priest, sat up in bed, looked to the window,
and peeled his tangerine, silently.

## *Peachstone*

I do not visit his grave. He is not there.
Out of hearing, out of reach. I miss him here,
seeing hair grease at the back of a chair
near a firegrate where his spit sizzled,
or noting, in the cut-glass bowl, a peach.

For that night his wife brought him a peach,
his favourite fruit, while the sick light glowed,
and his slack, dry mouth sucked, sucked, sucked,
with dying eyes closed – perhaps for her sake –
till bright as blood the peachstone showed.

## In the theatre

*(A true incident)*

*Only a local anaesthetic was given because of the blood-pressure problem. The patient, thus, was fully awake throughout the operation. But in those days – in 1938, in Cardiff, when I was Lambert Rogers' dresser – they could not locate a brain tumour with precision. Too much normal brain tissue was destroyed as the surgeon crudely searched for it, before he felt the resistance of it . . . all somewhat hit and miss. One operation I shall never forget . . .*

(Dr Wilfred Abse)

Sister saying – 'Soon you'll be back in the ward,'
sister thinking – 'Only two more on the list,'
the patient saying – 'Thank you, I feel fine';
small voices, small lies, nothing untoward,
though, soon, he would blink again and again
because of the fingers of Lambert Rogers,
rash as a blind man's, inside his soft brain.

If items of horror can make a man laugh
then laugh at this: one hour later, the growth
still undiscovered, ticking its own wild time;
more brain mashed because of the probe's braille path;
Lambert Rogers desperate, fingering still;
his dresser thinking, 'Christ! Two more on the list,
a cisternal puncture and a neural cyst.'

Then, suddenly, the cracked record in the brain,
a ventriloquist voice that cried, 'You sod,
leave my soul alone, leave my soul alone,' –
the patient's dummy lips moving to that refrain,

the patient's eyes too wide. And, shocked,
Lambert Rogers drawing out the probe
with nurses, students, sister, petrified.

'Leave my soul alone, leave my soul alone,'
that voice so arctic and that cry so odd
had nowhere else to go – till the antique
gramophone wound down and the words began
to blur and slow, '. . . leave . . . my . . . soul . . . alone . . .'
to cease at last when something other died.
And silence matched the silence under snow.

## Mysteries

At night, I do not know who I am
when I dream, when I am sleeping.

Awakened, I hold my breath and listen:
a thumbnail scratches the other side of the wall.

At midday, I enter a sunlit room
to observe the lamplight on for no reason.

I should know by now that few octaves can be heard,
that a vision dies from being too long stared at;

that the whole of recorded history even
is but a little gossip in a great silence;

that a magnesium flash cannot illumine,
for one single moment, the invisible.

I do not complain. I start with the visible
and am startled by the visible.

# D. J. ENRIGHT

# The Laughing Hyena, after Hokusai

For him, it seems, everything was molten. Court-ladies
    flow in gentle streams,
Or, gathering lotus, strain sideways from their curving
    boat,
A donkey prances, or a kite dances in the sky, or soars
    like sacrificial smoke.
All is flux: waters fall and leap, and bridges leap and fall.
Even his Tortoise undulates, and his Spring Hat is lively
    as a pool of fish.
All he ever saw was sea: a sea of marble splinters –
Long bright fingers claw across his pages, fjords and
    islands and shattered trees –

And the Laughing Hyena, cavalier of evil, as volcanic as
    the rest:
Elegant in a flowered gown, a face like a bomb-burst,
Featured with fangs and built about a rigid laugh,
Ever moving, like a pond's surface where a corpse has
    sunk.

Between the raised talons of the right hand rests an object –
At rest, like a pale island in a savage sea – a child's head,
Immobile, authentic, torn and bloody –
The point of repose in the picture, the point of movement
    in us.

Terrible enough, this demon. Yet it is present and perfect,
Firm as its horns, curling among its thick and handsome
    hair.
I find it an honest visitant, even consoling, after all

Those sententious phantoms, choked with rage and
    uncertainty,
Who grimace from contemporary pages. It, at least,
Knows exactly why it laughs.

## Prime Minister

Slowly he ticks off their names
On the long list:
All the young political men.

As he was once himself.
He thinks of how he despised the others
    – the a-political,
      the English-educated,
        the students he called 'white ants
In their ivory tower'.

Not so long ago, in fact,
He coined that happy phrase 'white ants'.
How he despised them, all they cared for
Was lectures, essays and a good degree!

A small thing these days
    – he tells himself –
To be arrested.
Incredulously he remembers
Not once was he arrested, somehow.

Slowly he ticks off the names
On the list to be arrested.
Tonight, isn't it? Yes,
Between 2 and 4 when the blood runs slow.
The young political men,
Full of fire, hot-blooded.
– For a moment,
He thinks he sees his own name there.
'Red ants,' he hisses,
Thrusting the list at a waiting policeman.

## *Brush-fire*

In a city of small pleasures, small spoils, small powers,
The wooden shacks are largely burning.
Bodies of small people lie along the shabby streets,
An old palace is smouldering.
Pushing bicycles piled with small bundles,
Families stream from north to south,
From south to north.

Who are these who are fighting those,
Fellow countrymen if not fellow men?
Some follow Prince X, some General Y.
Does Prince X lead the nobility, then,
And General Y the military?
Prince X is not particularly noble,
General Y is not so very military.
Some follow the Prince, for name's sake,
Or family's, or because he is there.
Some follow the General, for last month's pay,
Or family's sake, or because he walks in front.

Princes and generals have moderate ambitions.
An air-conditioned palace, a smarter G.H.Q.,
An Armstrong-Siddeley, another little wife.
The families, driven by some curious small ambition,
Stream away, from east to west, from west to east.
It is in their blood, to stream.
They know what is happening. None of them asks why –
They see that foreign tanks are running off with native
    drivers,

Foreign howitzers are manning native gunners –
As they pass by burning houses, on their way to burning
houses.
Among such small people, the foreign shells
Make ridiculously big noises.

## Children killed in War

A still day here,
Trees standing like a lantern show,
Cicadas, those sparse eaters, at their song,
The eye of silence, lost in soundlessness.

And then, no warning given,
Or if foreseen, then not to be escaped,
A well-aimed wind explodes,
And limbs of trees, which cannot run away,
May only hide behind each other.

Grant their death came promptly there,
Who died too soon,
That pain of parting was not long,
Roots ready to let fall their leaves.

The wind burns out,
The trees, what's left, resume their stand,
The singers stilled, an iron comb
Wrenched roughly through their lives.

While you, your thinking blown off course,
Design some simple windless heaven
Of special treats and toys,
Like picnic snapshots,
Like a magic-lantern show.

## The Monuments of Hiroshima

The roughly estimated ones, who do not sort well with
    our common phrases,
Who are by no means eating roots of dandelion,
    Or pushing up the daisies.

The more or less anonymous, to whom no human idiom
    can apply,
Who neither passed away, nor on, nor went before, nor
    vanished on a sigh.

Little of peace for them to rest in, less of them to rest in
    peace:
Dust to dust a swift transition, ashes to ash with awful
    ease.

Their only monument will be of others' casting –
A Tower of Peace, a Hall of Peace, a Bridge of Peace
    – who might have wished for something lasting,
Like a wooden box.

## In the Catalogue

It was a foreign horror.
A cold and lonely hour,
A place waste and littered,
And this figure standing there.

Like at first a prized
Cherry sapling swathed in straw.
It was no tree. It was enclosed
In a straw cocoon, and

Wore a hood of sacking
Over the might-be head
And the should-be shoulders.
It seemed to be looking.

What did I fear the most?
To ignore and bustle past?
To acknowledge and perhaps
Find out what best was lost?

It didn't accost. I did.
Rattling in my outstretched hand,
I hoped that money would talk,
A language of the land.

Some inner motion stirred the straw.
My stomach turned, I waited
For its – what? – its rustling claw
Or something I could not conceive.

What happened was the worst.
Nothing. Or simply, the straw
Subsided. 'Please, please!'
I begged. But nothing more.

Fear is glad to turn to anger.
I threw the money down and left,
Heedless of any danger,
Aside from vomiting.

From twenty yards I turned
To look. The shape stood still.
Another ten yards, and I strained
My eyes on icy shadows –

The shape was scrabbling for my coins!
I thanked my stomach. Then
Thanked God, who'd left the thing
Enough to make a man.

## *I was a gulli-gulli man's chicken*

Come to terms with one's environment, you say?
Grass, grit and weather should be my environment:
I find myself a card, any card, in any pack of cards.

My master cannot do more than he can do.
(The greatest of beings suffers his own limitations.)
My master has almost come to terms with his environment.

Which means: Be startling but not shocking.
Be funny but clean. Be efficient but seem kindly.
He walks a tightrope. The tightrope is me.

Passed under summer frocks, I fight with elastic;
Planted in large bosoms, I beat my head on brassières;
Marooned on barren waists, I skate on whalebone.

Do you know what human flesh smells like, as the
Whole of one's environment? The stuffiness of cotton,
The uncertainty of silk, the treachery of nylon?

Do you know that on the first-class deck, P & O,
My anus is lightly sewn up? The greatest of beings
Must please most of the people most of the time.

My master is all for cleanliness. How much
Cleanliness can a small animal like me endure?
How much being lost, do you think? How much handling?

They have invented toys which look like us.
It's little wonder that we living creatures
Should be held as toys. But cheaper, cheaper.

So I have come to terms with my environment.
Which is: hands that grasp me like a wheel or lever,
And an early (but at least organic) disappearance.

## *Parliament of Cats*

The cats caught a Yellow-vented Bulbul.
Snatched from them, for three days it uttered
Its gentle gospel, enthroned above their heads.
Became loved and respected of all the cats.
Then succumbed to internal injuries.
The cats regretted it all profoundly,
They would never forget the wrong they had done.

Later the cats caught a Daurian Starling.
And ate it. For a Daurian Starling is not
A Yellow-vented Bulbul. (Genuflection.)
Its colouring is altogether different.
It walks in a different, quite unnatural fashion.
The case is not the same at all as that of
The Yellow-vented Bulbul. (Genuflection.)

The kittens caught a Yellow-vented Bulbul.
And ate it. What difference, they ask, between
A Yellow-vented Bulbul and that known criminal
The Daurian Starling? Both move through the air
In a quite unnatural fashion. This is not
The Yellow-vented Bulbul of our parents' day,
Who was a Saint of course! (Genuflection.)

# Small Hotel

Not *Guest* –
The Chinese, those corrected souls, all know
A guest is never billed, whereas the
Essence of my aspect is, I pay –

But *Occupier*. Good words cost no more.
*The Occupier is hereby kindly warned,*
*It is forbidden strictly by the Law*
– In smudged ungainly letters on his door –
*Not to introduce into this room*
*Prostitutes and gambling, and instruments of*
*Opium Smoking and spitting on the floor.*

*By Order*, all the lot, *The Management.*
The Chinese have immense respect for Order,
They manage anything you name, except

To keep their voices down. Outside my door
The Management all night obeys the Law,
Gambles and introduces prostitutes,
And spits upon the floor and kicks around
The instruments of opium smoking.

It is forbidden to the Occupier
To sleep, or introduce into his room
Dreams, or the instruments of restoration.
He finds he has his work cut strictly out
To meet the mandates of the Law and Order.

Coffee, frying garlic and a sudden calm
Imply the onset of a working day.
Kings and queens and jacks have all departed,
Mosquitoes nurse their bloody hangovers.

So large a bill of fare, so small the bill!
A yawning boy bears off my lightweight bag,
Sins of omission make my heavier load.
Insulting gringo. Cultural-imperialist.

Maybe a liberal tip will mollify
The Law, the Order, and the Management? –
With what I leave behind on that hard bed:
Years off my life, a century of rage
And envy.

D. J. ENRIGHT

# Kyoto in Autumn

Precarious hour. Moment of charity and the less usual
    love.
Mild evening. Even taxis now fall mild.
Grey heart, grey city, grey and dusty dove.

Retiring day peers back through paper windows; here
    and there a child
Digs long-lost treasure from between her feet.

Where yesterday the sun's staff beat, where winter's
    claws tomorrow sink,
The silent ragman picks his comfort now.

The straitened road holds early drunkards like a
    stronger vow;
The season's tang renews the burning tongue.

Poetic weather, nowhere goes unsung,
However short the song. A pipe's smoke prints
Its verses on the hand-made paper of that sky;

And under lanterns leaping like struck flints, a potter's
    novice squats
And finds his colours in the turning air.

A pallid grace invests the gliding cars.
The Kamo keeps its decent way, not opulent nor bare.
The last light waves a fading hand. Now fiercer seasons
    start like neon in the little bars.

## Am Steinplatz

Benches round a square of grass.
You enter by the stone that asks,
      'Remember those whom Hitlerism killed'.
'Remember those whom Stalinism killed',
Requests the stone by which you leave.

This day, as every other day,
I shuffle through the little park,
      from stone to stone,
From conscience-cancelling stone to stone,
Peering at the fading ribbons on the faded wreaths.

At least the benches bear their load,
Of people reading papers, eating ices,
Watching aeroplanes and flowers,
Sleeping, smoking, counting, cuddling.
      Everything but heed those stony words.
They have forgotten. As they must.
Remember those who live. Yes, they are right.
      They must.

A dog jumps on the bench beside me.
Nice doggie: never killed a single Jew, or Gentile.
Then it jumps on me. Its paws are muddy, muzzle wet.
Gently I push it off. It likes this game of war.

At last a neat stout lady on a nearby bench
Calls tenderly, 'Komm, Liebchen, komm!
Der Herr' – this public-park-frau barks –
      'does not like dogs!'

Shocked papers rustle to the ground;
Ices drip away forgotten; sleepers wake;
The lovers mobilize their distant eyes.
     The air strikes cold.
There's no room for a third stone here.
     I leave.

## Displaced Person looks at a Cage-bird

Every single day, going to where I stay
      (how long?), I pass the canary
In the window. Big bird, all pranked out,
Looming and booming in the window's blank.

Closing a pawky eye, tapping its hairy chest,
      flexing its brawny wing.
Every single day, coming from where I stay
(How long?), I pass this beastly thing.

How I wish it were dead!
      – Florid, complacent, rent-free and over-fed,
Feather-bedded, pensioned, free from wear and tear,
Earth has not anything to show less fair.

I do wish it were dead!
      Then I'd write a better poetry,
On that poor wee bird, its feet in the air,
An innocent victim of something. Just like me.

# Broken Fingernails: Japan 1953

A shabby old man is mixing water with clay.
If that shabby old man had given up hope
(He is probably tired: he has worked all day)
The flimsy house would never have been built.

If the flimsy house had never been built
Six people would shiver in the autumn breath.
If thousands of shabby old men were sorry as you
Millions of people would cough themselves to death.

(In the town the pin-ball parlours sing like cicadas)
Do not take refuge in some far-off foreign allusion
(In the country the cicadas ring like pin-ball parlours)
Simply remark the clay, the water, the straw, and a
    useful person.

## A Superstition

Dangerous to laugh at butterflies!
Who seem more simple than they are,
Partake of worms and birds and bats
And Rorschach blots and tapestries;
Are intimate with breezes
And the inner life of flowers
And sensuous forests sealed to us;
Who know that laughs beget like rabbits
And end in breaking more than butterflies
On worse than wheels.

Blame, if we will, the weals
They raise on hapless cabbages,
Their way of bringing up their young
(Exposed to beaks or cosseted in silks),
Their lack of *Tiefe*, all their peacocks
Nibbling at carrion, who call it nectar.
We'll say our say,
We'd make a feeble sort of butterfly,
We'd better try to stay a man.

And teach them what we can, as man to man:
Their world is not averse to missionaries
(Baths for Birds,
Gale Warnings for Winged Insects,
Chiropody for Centipedes).
Such uses they are glad to learn,
They know themselves more beautiful than we,
As men to flies.

But dangerous to laugh at butterflies!
They're growing bigger every year.

# *In Memoriam*

How clever they are, the Japanese, how clever!
The great department store, Takashimaya, on the
Ginza, near Maruzen Bookshop and British Council –
A sky-scraper swaying with every earth-tremor,
Bowing and scraping, but never falling (how clever!).
On the roof-garden of tall Takashimaya lives an
Elephant. How did he get there, that clever Japanese
Elephant? By lift? By helicopter? (How clever,
Either way.) And this young man who went there to teach
(Uncertificated, but they took him) in Tokyo,
This Englishman with a fine beard and a large and
(It seemed) a healthy body.

                         And he married an orphan,
A Japanese orphan (illegitimate child of
A *geisha* – Japanese for 'a clever person' – and a
Number of customers), who spoke no English and
He spoke no Japanese. (But how clever they were!)
For a year they were married. She said, half in Japanese,
Half in English, wholly in truth: 'This is the first time
I have known happiness.' (The Japanese are a
Clever people, clever but sad.) 'They call it a
Lottery,' he wrote to me, 'I have made a lucky dip.'
(She was a Japanese orphan, brought up in a convent.)
At the end of that year he started to die.
They flew him to New York, for 2-million volt treatment
('Once a day,' he wrote, 'Enough to make you sick!')
And a number of operations. 'They say there's a
90% chance of a cure,' he wrote, 'Reversing
The odds, I suspect.' Flying back to his orphan,
He was removed from the plane at Honolulu and
Spent four days in a slummy hotel with no money or

Clothes. His passport was not in order. (Dying men
Are not always clever enough in thinking ahead.)
They operated again in Tokyo and again,
He was half a man, then no man, but the cancer
Throve on it. 'All I can say is,' he wrote in November,
'Takashimaya will damned well have to find
Another Father Christmas this year, that's all.'
(It was. He died a week later. I was still puzzling
How to reply.)
               He would have died anywhere.
And he lived his last year in Japan, loved by a
Japanese orphan, teaching her the rudiments of
Happiness, and (without certificate) teaching
Japanese students. In the dungeons of learning, the
Concentration campuses, crammed with ragged uniforms
And consumptive faces, in a land where the literacy
Rate is over 100%, and the magazines
Read each other in the crowded subways. And
He was there (clever of them!), he was there teaching.
Then she went back to her convent, the Japanese
Widow, having known a year's happiness with a
Large blue-eyed red-bearded foreign devil, that's all.
There is a lot of cleverness in the world, but still
Not enough.

D. J. ENRIGHT

## Dreaming in the Shanghai Restaurant

I would like to be that elderly Chinese gentleman.
He wears a gold watch with a gold bracelet,
But a shirt without sleeves or tie.
He has good-luck moles on his face, but is not
        disfigured with fortune.
His wife resembles him, but is still a handsome woman,
She has never bound her feet or her belly.
Some of the party are his children, it seems,
And some his grandchildren;
No generation appears to intimidate another.
He is interested in people, without wanting to
        convert them or pervert them.
He eats with gusto, but not with lust;
And he drinks, but is not drunk.
He is content with his age, which has always suited him.
When he discusses a dish with the pretty waitress,
It is the dish he discusses, not the waitress.
The table-cloth is not so clean as to show indifference,
Not so dirty as to signify a lack of manners.
He proposes to pay the bill but knows he will not be
        allowed to.
He walks to the door like a man who doesn't fret
        about being respected, since he is;
A daughter or granddaughter opens the door for him,
And he thanks her.
It has been a satisfying evening. Tomorrow
Will be a satisfying morning. In between
        he will sleep satisfactorily.
I guess that for him it is peace in his time.
It would be agreeable to be this Chinese gentleman.

## Another person one would like to be

Is a 19th-century composer of
Masses for the Dead.
God knows, one has the emotions anyway
One might as well believe in them.

No call to concoct a plot
No need to write the words
No lack of occasion –
There are masses of dead.

Once I wished I were an old Chinese gentleman
Glimpsed in a Chinese restaurant
Amid masses of Chinese relatives –
With the years one's ambitions grow humbler.

## *Sightseeing*

Along the long wide temple wall
Extends a large and detailed painting.

A demon's head, its mouth square open,
Inside the mouth a room of people squatting.

Its fangs the polished pillars of the room,
The crimson carpet of the floor its tongue.

Inside this room a painting on the wall,
A demon's head, its mouth square open.

Inside the mouth a room of people squatting,
Their faces blank, the artist did not care.

Inside that room a painting on the wall,
A demon's head, its mouth square open.

Somewhere you are squatting, somewhere there.
Imagination, like the eyes that strain

Against the wall, is happily too weak
To number all the jaws there are to slip.

## Come to Sunny S

You step down over the silvery sea,
Under the blue air, and there you find
The roads are rather Roman, and Guinness
Is served ice-cold in the wine-shops,
That the buildings are modern, or else
Middle-aged, no older than you are.

The British have left GO–CAUTION–STOP
At intersections. Park opposite a
White line, you will surely be fined.
No mystery, simply a white line, a fine.
The laws are rather Roman too.

There are no *nautch* girls here,
No *geisha*, no sing-song girls, indeed
We have nothing along those lines except
Girls.

Our temples were erected yesterday,
And renovated this morning. We see no
Virtue in decay. Our schools face the old
Problem: children. Our scent is chiefly
Petrol. Our shops sell what we need.

Among our customs, self-sacrifice to
Tourists is not one. We sell you
What you can get at Harrods or Liberty's
But, being the East, a little cheaper.

We do not sell virgins cheap,
We need them. If you prick us, we shall
Probably bleed. For a price you can get
What you can get at home for a price.
We are not certain what we are, we are
Various. You will write books later and
Tell us. We shall display your books
In our tourist hotels.

Our speciality is race riots: which
Wouldn't interest you half as much as
The forbidden dances of temple prostitutes
(Tickets sold at all Government offices)
Or the Spring Festival (held every Saturday)
Of a special class of female artist –
Neither of which we have in this country.

Our speciality is human trouble:
Which mightn't appeal to you, seeing
You could get your heads, breasts or
Balls sliced off accidentally. This
Is our only form of human sacrifice.

And I tell you this because I think
You may be human.

## *J.T. on his Travels*

Perhaps you thought she was a child
Perhaps you thought you liked the thought

She doesn't pretend to be a virgin
Her son is lying on the only bed

Almost her size, she carries him
Still sleeping to a next-door cupboard

She brings a bucket of water back
To give herself a local wash

You feel you prefer your own french letter
Hers look second-hand

You she will wash hereafter
If you last that long

Either way you are damned –
If you manage, for unfeelingness

If you don't, for lack of feeling
John Thomas, old Whitey, you can't win.

## Cats and Dogs

One has lived too long perhaps
In a country without cats,
Where the dogs strut by the fence
To keep far hence
The poor man, madman and the thief.

One has lived too long perhaps
In a land of cold-eyed cats,
Where no dogs go
With teeth and tail and tongue to show
Our woes are not unique.

## Nature Poetry

I was regarding the famous trees, locked in the case
Of a glassy sky, as dignified as some dead face,
As dead as well.
                    Until my daughter scampered up, gabbling
Of the famous monkeys in the zoo. And the trees were
    suddenly scrabbling
In the air, they glowed, they shook with communal rage.
For the trees were bereaved of monkeys. And in the zoo
The bitter monkeys shook the dead iron of their cage.

## *Making Love*

Making love –
Love was what they'd made.
In rooms here and there,
In this town and that.
Something they had made –
Children to a childless pair.

Meeting now to unmake love,
To send this invitee
Who'd overstepped the bounds
Back where he belonged
(Though where did he belong?),
Easy come, they said, he'd easy go.

But love was what they'd made;
Acts turned to things.
These children of a childless pair
Had quickly put on weight,
And now stood round:
'Easier to make us than unmake.'

Such towering children they had made,
Not to be mislaid in hotel corridors,
Or shaken off in trains, or sleep.
And thus walled in,
What move could two small mortals make? –
Except make love.

## The Afterlife

Wicked in hand and eye, this knowing arab
Buys, with a stolen stylo, a sweet and scented beverage.
He squats outside the café, and in melting sun
Admires the brown legs of the ladies, and the ocean's
    frilly edge.

This worthy clerk, whose pen makes others rich,
Shivers in the nameless steam, behind the swaying
    swinging door.
His hard-earned shilling gains a wet and windy snack.
The rain strikes down, the smoke fights back,
His bus is late once more.

But after life there comes, as this suggests, an afterlife.
The arab shall repent his careless crimes in one long dirty
    draught
In some eternal midland town. The honest clerk,
Beside a varnished sea, be lulled for ever on a swaying raft,
And chew *soudani*, garnished with dancing girls and waves.

## Metropolitan Water Bawd

The use of a hose
For non-domestic purposes
Can be quite costly.

And even more so
If an automatic sprinkler is employed,
Which goes without saying, and similarly
A perforated hose.

The hose should be held in the hand throughout
And the fittings must comply with the by-laws
And statutory requirements of the Bawd.

When a hose is in use, the flow
Should not be left to run unattended,
Otherwise you are liable.
The apparatus should be supported
Clear of the ground, using both hands
If necessary. Otherwise you are liable.

For remember: the conditions applicable
To domestic usage at private residences
Do not apply to non-domestic purposes
(Whether in private residences or public places)
Involving a hose, tube, pipe, sprinkler
Or whatever endearment you choose to employ.

For such usages there will be extra charges
Which may be paid in advance or subsequently
Or both.

But if you no longer desire to use a hose
Or if changed circumstances have rendered
Continued use inapplicable
Please delete the charge from your account
By detaching the portion and duly returning it.

## Since Then

So many new crimes since then! –

    simple simony
    manducation of corpses
    infringement of copyright
    offences against the sumptuary laws
    postlapsarian undress
    violation of the Hay-Pauncefote Treaty
    extinction of the dodo
    champerty and malversation
    travelling by public transport without a ticket
    hypergamy and other unnatural practices
    courting in bed
    free verse
    wilful longevity
    dumb insolence
    bootlegging and hijacking
    jackbooting and highlegging
    arsenic and old lace
    robbing a hen-roost
    leaving unattended bombs in unauthorized places
    high dudgeon
    the cod war
    massacre of innocents
    bed-wetting
    escapism
    transporting Bibles without a licence

But so many new punishments, too! –

    blinding with science
    death by haranguing

licking of envelopes
palpation of the obvious
invasion of the privacies
fistula in ano
hard labour down the minds
solitary conjunction
mortification of the self-esteem
the Plastic Maiden
hat-rack and trouser-press
the death of a thousand budgerigars
spontaneous combustion
self-employment
retooling of the economy
jacks in orifice
boredom of the genitals
trampling by white elephants
deprivation of forgetfulness
loss of pen-finger
severance pay
strap-hanging
early closing
sequestration of the funny-bone
mortgage and deadlock

'Fair do's,' murmured the old Adam, 'I am well pleased.'
He had come a long way since he named the animals.

## The Cauldron

> *it is the time when uprightly and in pious sober wise, naught of work is to be wrought and art grown unpossible without the divel's help and fires of hell under the cauldron . . .*

It had grown impossible
Very little work was getting done.
So we gave up sobriety
The other virtues as well
(We supposed that once we had them)
And we stoked the fires of hell.

How we stoked them! It was fun at first
At first there were virgins to astound
There were things to be done with things
There were things to be done in private
There were things to be done in public
At first.

It was style we believed in, not the devil
It was the devil we got.
The fires of hell are not for hire
Without the ice.
There was a saying about the devil . . .
But memory has gone, we killed it
A package deal.

Now there is no one to astound
The devil only laughs at his own jokes
Us he finds boring.
There is nothing to do in public
Nothing to do in private.
Under the dry cauldron icy fires are burning
Art is grown impossible.

Where is the future? Nothing stirring
Unless a memory stirs.
Wasn't there an ancient saying . . .
About a time when uprightly alone
In pious sober wise can work be done
And with the devil's hindrance?

## Ghosts

Our ghosts were always white.
How would you tell them, otherwise,
    by night?
Like pale sheets floating into sight,
They glow with silent light.

There will be other ghosts these days.
Change comes in all our ways.
And they are black, for darkness has
    its rays.
Ghosts of the noontide blaze.

## It is Poetry

As Leverkühn began his last address
To the cultivated ladies and gentlemen
There assembled,
They were highly bewildered.

Till one of them cried,
'Why, it is poetry! One is hearing poetry!'
Thus relieving them all immensely.

But not for long –
As the composer's friend noted –
Alas, not for long did one think so!
They were hearing about damnation.

It sent the speaker mad.
The listeners it sent home indignant.
They had expected an artistic soirée.

## *Said the Straw*

'It's the last camel,' said the straw,
'The last camel that breaks our backs.'

'Consider the lilies,' he said,
'How they toil in the fields.
Six days they labour,
On Sunday they wear their best clothes.'

'Ask why the violet sickened,
The pale primrose died unmarried,
And the daisy lies in chains,'
He said, 'All grass is flesh.'

'But let us hear no more,'
So said the straw,
'About the sorrows of the camel
With its huge and heavy feet.'

## Home and Colonial:
## Or, Rousseau's Tropical Storm with Tiger

I'm not one of those simpletons who believe
That if only they had a larger TV screen
They would be able to see the naughty bits.
But if that picture were a few inches longer,
Here, on the right-hand side, I mean – then
In fact you would see – not a naughty bit –
You would see me.

Sexual behaviour does exist in the tropics –
Oh indeed – but it's relatively invisible.
It doesn't go on in public. And it wouldn't
Even if there weren't a storm, even if
The jungle weren't so full of spiky things.

Public sex is less sex than public, I reckon.
Like that young couple in the Underground
The other night. They weren't doing anything,
They were simulating it. In my day
We used to dissimulate. And likewise I doubt
This notion that a wider screen induces
A broader mind. What you can see is never
The interesting part. Though of course
I'm not referring to a gentleman like you
Looking at a picture like this
In a reputable gallery.

Imagination is allowed some latitude,
I know (though, as it happens, this painting
Doesn't get enough), but all the same . . .
The jungle's not half as pretty as it looks here,

Untidy at the best, storm or no storm.
The bougainvillæa was tatty and blotched,
Not just out of a hot-house. It was gloomy –
That's another thing about jungles – and
The lightning had that lost air it always has
In those parts. Fumbling around for something
To get a grip on, like a roof, a chimney
Or a golf club.

But the tiger – Frenchy's hit it off to a T!
Scared stiff, what with its tail behind, which it
Took for a flying snake, and in front – a hairy
Red-faced white man in a post-impressionist sarong,
Heading for the nearest *kedai*.
I fancied an ice-cold Guinness. A moment later
And there'd have been just me on that canvas,
Dry and wet at once, sarong slipping a bit,
Tiger a mile away and still running.

Even so, would you really see more on a larger
  screen,
D'you think? Or do the girls wear towels or
  something?

## Goodbye Empire

It had to go
So many wounded feelings
And some killings –
In a nutshell, too expensive

Though its going
Scarcely set its subjects free
For freedom –
Life still exacts a fee

In wounded feelings
And also killings
Slates wiped clean
Soon attract new chalkings

At least the old régime
Allowed its odd anomalies
Like my orphaned Irish dad
One of those Wild Geese

Who floundered over India
In the shit and out of it
Getting a stripe, and then
Falling off his horse and losing it.

## The Ancient Anthropologist

Let me tell you how it happened. Once
I had my finger on the pulse,
The pulse of a large and noteworthy people.

This pulse was a pile-driver, a pounder
On golden gates and coffin lids, a grinder
Of organs, a kraken, a jetstream of tears.

Believe me, it was swings and Ferris wheels,
Switchbacks and Ghost Trains and Walls
Of Death, dodgems and multifarious booths.

I dug in my heels, hung on by my nails.
Till 'Hands off!' thundered that great pulse,
Though not so great as not to notice me.

Perhaps it misconceived my fingers pressed
Concupiscently? Or set to twist its wrist?
– Activities that fall outside my field.

That was long ago. Today I'm as you find me.
All my articulations flapping freely,
Free from every prejudice, shaking all over.

## Along the River

They had pulled her out of the river. She was dead,
Lying against the rhododendrons sewn with spider's
    thread.
An oldish woman, in a shabby dress, a straggling stocking,
A worn, despairing face. How could the old do such a
    thing?

Now forty years have passed. Again I recall that poor
Thing laid along the River Leam, and I look once more.

They have pulled her out of the river. She is dead,
Lying against the rhododendrons sewn with spider's
    thread.
A youngish woman, in a sodden dress, a straggling
    stocking,
A sad, appealing face. How can the young do such a thing?

# How Many Devils Can Dance on the Point...

### 1

Why, this is hell,
And we are in it.
It began with mysterious punishments
And the punishments led to the crimes
Which are currently being punished.
The more rational you are
(What you have paid for
You will expect to obtain
Without further payment)
The less your chances of remission.
Only the insane and saintly
Who kiss the rod so hard they break it
Escape to a palliated hell.
For the rest, why, this is it,
And we are in it.

### 2

Then what of those
Whose punishment was such, they
Never lived to carry out their crimes?
Children, say,
More than whose fingers were held
For more than a second in more than
The flame of a candle;
Though not exclusively children.
(No need to draw a picture for you:
The chamber, the instruments, the torture;
Forget the unimaginable, the

Imaginable suffices for present purposes.)
If the other was hell
Then what is this? –
There are gradations of Hades
Like the Civil Service,
Whereby the first is paradise
Compared with the last;
And heaven is where we are
When we think of where we might have been.
(Except that when we think,
We are in hell.)

3

Can this be heaven
Where a thoughtful landlord
Locates the windows of his many mansions
To afford you such a view?
(The chamber, the instruments, the torture.)
Can it be
The gratifying knowledge of having pleased
Someone who derives such pleasure
From being thus gratified?

4

Moves, then,
In a mysterious way . . .
Except that –
Lucid, strict and certain,
Shining, wet and hard,
No mystery at all.
Why, this is hell.

## The Wine List

> *— And Paradiso? Is there a*
> *paradise?*
> *— I think so, madam,*
> *but nobody wants sweet wines*
> *any more.*
>
> Eugenio Montale, translated
> by G. Singh

Not so fast, waiter.
If there are those who like sweet wine
And have earned the price of it,
Then they should have it.

Plonk will do for me.
If there's cork in it
Or lipstick on the rim,
I shan't make a fuss.
Some of us will be lucky to get vinegar
Pushed at us.

But for others
You had better be ready to serve sweet wine
In clean glasses, unchipped,
And without a speech.
Some customers are by definition
Right,
As it happens,
And do not require to be told
About a fine dry wine
Deriving from individually crushed grapes
Grown on a certain slope on a small hill
Overlooking a distinguished river.

Some of your customers
Have already been individually crushed.
They know dryness in the mouth,
A harsh taste at the back of the throat.
If sweet wine is what they fancy
You will give them sweet wine.

And there should be room on your tray
For ginger-beer, orangeade, cocoa, tea
And even the vulgar vintage of colas.

# Poet Wondering What He Is Up To

– A sort of extra hunger,
Less easy to assuage than some
– Or else an extra ear

Listening for a telephone,
Which might or might not ring
In a distant room

– Or else a fear of ghosts
And fear lest ghosts might not appear,
Double superstition, double fear

– To miss and miss and miss,
And then to have, and still to know
That you must miss and miss anew

– It almost sounds like love,
Love in an early stage,
The thing you're talking of

– (but Beauty – no,
Problems of Leisure – no,
Maturity – hardly so)

– And this? Just metaphors
Describing metaphors describing – what?
The eccentric circle of your years.

# MICHAEL LONGLEY

## Epithalamion

These are the small hours when
Moths by their fatal appetite
That brings them tapping to get in,
    Are steered along the night
To where our window catches light.

Who hazard all to be
Where we, the only two it seems,
Inhabit so delightfully
    A room it bursts its seams
And spills on to the lawn in beams,

Such visitors as these
Reflect with eyes like frantic stars
This garden's brightest properties,
    Cruising its corridors
Of light above the folded flowers,

Till our vicinity
Is rendered royal by their flight
Towards us, till more silently
    The silent stars ignite,
Their aeons dwindling by a night,

And everything seems bent
On robing in this evening you
And me, all dark the element
    Our light is earnest to,
All quiet gathered round us who,

When over the embankments
A train that's loudly reprobate
Shoots from silence into silence,
    With ease accommodate
Its pandemonium, its freight.

I hold you close because
We have decided dark will be
For ever like this and because,
    My love, already
The dark is growing elderly.

With dawn upon its way,
Punctually and as a rule,
The small hours widening into day,
    Our room its vestibule
Before it fills all houses full,

We too must hazard all,
Switch off the lamp without a word
For the last of night assembled
    Over it and unperturbed
By the moth that lies there littered,

And notice how the trees
Which took on anonymity
Are again in their huge histories
    Displayed, that wherever we
Attempt, and as far as we can see,

The flowers everywhere
Are withering, the stars dissolved,
Amalgamated in a glare,
    Which last night were revolved
Discreetly round us – and, involved,

The two of us, in these
Which early morning has deformed,
Must hope that in new properties
    We'll find a uniform
To know each other truly by, or,

    At the least, that these will,
When we rise, be seen with dawn
As remnant yet part raiment still,
    Like flags that linger on
The sky when king and queen are gone.

## No Continuing City

My hands here, gentle, where her breasts begin,
My picture in her eyes –
It is time for me to recognize
This new dimension, my last girl.
So, to set my house in order, I imagine
Photographs, advertisements – the old lies,
The lumber of my soul –

All that is due for spring-cleaning,
Everything that soul-destroys.
Into the open I bring
Girls who linger still in photostat
(For whom I was so many different boys) –
I explode their myths before it is too late,
Their promises I detonate –

There is quite a lot that I can do . . .
I leave them – are they six or seven, two or three? –
Locked in their small geographies.
The hillocks of their bodies' lovely shires
(Whose all weathers I have walked through)
Acre by acre recede entire
To summer country.

From collision to eclipse their case is closed.
Who took me by surprise
Like comets first – now, failing to ignite,
They constellate such uneventful skies,
Their stars arranged each night
In the old stories
Which I successfully have diagnosed.

Though they momentarily survive
In my delays,
They neither cancel nor improve
My continuing city with old ways,
Familiar avenues to love –
Down my one-way streets (it is time to finish)
Their eager syllables diminish.

Though they call out from the suburbs
Of experience – they know how that disturbs! –
Or, already tending towards home,
Prepare to hitch-hike on the kerbs,
Their bags full of dear untruths –
I am their medium
And I take the words out of their mouths.

From today new hoardings crowd my eyes,
Pasted over my ancient histories
Which (I must be cruel to be kind)
Only gale or cloudburst now discover,
Ripping the billboard of my mind –
Oh, there my lovers,
There my dead no longer advertise.

I transmit from the heart a closing broadcast
To my girl, my bride, my wife-to-be –
I tell her she is welcome,
Advising her to make this last,
To be sure of finding room in me
(I embody bed and breakfast) –
To eat and drink me out of house and home.

# The Hebrides

## for Eavan Boland

### 1

The winds' enclosure, Atlantic's premises,
   Last balconies
  Above the waves, the Hebrides –
   Too long did I postpone
Presbyterian granite and the lack of trees,
   This orphaned stone

Day in, day out colliding with the sea.
   Weather forecast,
  Compass nor ordnance survey
   Arranges my welcome
For, on my own, I have lost my way at last,
   So far from home.

In whom the city is continuing,
   I stop to look,
  To find my feet among the ling
   And bracken – over me
The bright continuum of gulls, a rook
   Occasionally.

### 2

My eyes, slowly accepting panorama,
   Try to include
  In my original idea
   The total effect
Of air and ocean – waterlogged all wood –
   All harbours wrecked –

My dead-lights latched by whelk and barnacle
Till I abide
By the sea wall of the time I kill –
My each nostalgic scheme
Jettisoned, as crises are, the further side
Of sleep and dream.

Between wind and wave this holiday
The cormorant,
The oyster-catcher and osprey
Proceed and keep in line
While I, hands in my pockets, hesitant,
Am in two minds.

3

Old neighbours, though shipwreck's my decision,
People my brain –
Like breakwaters against the sun,
Command in silhouette
My island circumstance – my cells retain,
Perpetuate

Their crumpled deportment through bad weather,
And I feel them
Put on their raincoats for ever
And walk out in the sea.
I am, though each one waves a phantom limb,
The amputee,

For these are my sailors, these my drowned –
In their heart of hearts,
In their city I ran aground.
Along my arteries
Sluice those homewaters petroleum hurts.
Dry dock, gantries,

Dykes of apparatus educate my bones
To track the buoys
Up sea lanes love emblazons
To streets where shall conclude
My journey back from flux to poise, from poise
To attitude.

Here, at the edge of my experience,
Another tide
Along the broken shore extends
A lifetime's wrack and ruin –
No flotsam I may beachcomb now can hide
That water line.

4

Beyond the lobster pots where plankton spreads
Porpoises turn.
Seals slip over the cockle beds.
Undertow dishevels
Seaweed in the shallows – and I discern
My sea levels.

To right and left of me there intervene
The tumbled burns –
And these, on turf and boulder weaned,
Confuse my calendar –
Their tilt is suicidal, their great return
Curricular.

No matter what repose holds shore and sky
In harmony,
From this place in the long run I,
Though here I might have been
Content with rivers where they meet the sea,
Remove upstream,

Where the salmon, risking fastest waters –
Waterfall and rock
And the effervescent otters –
On bridal pools insist
As with fin and generation they unlock
The mountain's fist.


5


Now, buttoned up, with water in my shoes,
Clouds around me,
I can, through mist that misconstrues,
Read like a palimpsest
My past – those landmarks and that scenery
I dare resist.

Into my mind's unsympathetic trough
They fade away –
And to alter my perspective
I feel in the sharp cold
Of my vantage point too high above the bay
The sea grow old.

Granting the trawlers far below their stance,
Their anchorage,
I fight all the way for balance –
In the mountain's shadow
Losing foothold, covet the privilege
Of vertigo.

## *Circe*

The cries of the shipwrecked enter my head.
On wildest nights when the torn sky confides
Its face to the sea's cracked mirror, my bed
– Addressed by the moon and her tutored tides –

Through brainstorm, through nightmare and ocean
Keeps me afloat. Shallows are my coven,
The comfortable margins – in this notion
I stand uncorrected by the sun even.

Out of the night husband after husband
– Eyes wide as oysters, arms full of driftwood –
Wades ashore and puts in at my island.
My necklaces of seashells and seaweed,

My skirts of spindrift, sandals of flotsam
Catch the eye of each bridegroom for ever.
Quite forgetful of the widowing calm
My sailors wait through bad and good weather.

At first in rock pools I become their wife,
Under the dunes at last they lie with me –
These are the spring and neap tides of their life.
I have helped so many sailors off the sea,

And, counting no man among my losses,
I have made of my arms and my thighs last rooms
For the irretrievable and capsized –
I extend the sea, its idioms.

## Leaving Inishmore

Rain and sunlight and the boat between them
Shifted whole hillsides through the afternoon –
Quiet variations on an urgent theme
Reminding me now that we left too soon
The island awash in wave and anthem.

Miles from the brimming enclave of the bay
I hear again the Atlantic's voices,
The gulls above us as we pulled away –
So munificent their final noises
These are the broadcasts from our holiday.

Oh, the crooked walkers on that tilting floor!
And the girls singing on the upper deck
Whose hair took the light like a downpour –
Interim nor change of scene shall shipwreck
Those folk on the move between shore and shore.

Summer and solstice as the seasons turn
Anchor our boat in a perfect standstill,
The harbour wall of Inishmore astern
Where the Atlantic waters overspill –
I shall name this the point of no return

Lest that excursion out of light and heat
Take on a January idiom –
Our ocean icebound when the year is hurt,
Wintertime past cure – the curriculum
Vitae of sailors and the sick at heart.

## Dr Johnson on the Hebrides

for Philip Hobsbaum

The Hebridean gales mere sycophants,
So many loyal Boswells at his heel –
Yet the farflung outposts of experience
In the end undo a Roman wall,

The measured style. London is so far;
Each windswept strait he would encompass
Gives the unsinkable lexicographer
His reflection in its shattered glass.

He trudges off in the mist and the rain
Where only the thickest skin survives,
Among the rocks construes himself again,
Lifts through those altering perspectives

His downcast eyes, riding out the brainstorm,
His weatherproof enormous head at home.

## Journey out of Essex

*or, John Clare's Escape from the Madhouse*

I am lying with my head
Over the edge of the world,
Unpicking my whereabouts
Like the asylum's name
That they stitch on the sheets.

Sick now with bad weather
Or a virus from the fens,
I dissolve in a puddle
My biographies of birds
And the names of flowers.

That they may recuperate
Alongside the stunned mouse,
The hedgehog rolled in leaves,
I am putting to bed
In this rheumatic ditch

The boughs of my harvest-home,
My wives, one on either side,
And keeping my head low as
A lark's nest, my feet toward
Helpston and the pole star.

## Freeze-up

The freeze-up annexes the sea even,
Putting out over the waves its platform.
Let skies fall, the fox's belly cave in –
This catastrophic shortlived reform
Directs to our homes the birds of heaven.
They come on farfetched winds to keep us warm.

Bribing these with bounty, we would rather
Forget our hopes of thaw when spring will clean
The boughs, dust from our sills snow and feather,
Release to its decay and true decline
The bittern whom this different weather
Cupboarded in ice like a specimen.

## A Personal Statement

for Seamus Heaney

Since you, Mind, think to diagnose
Experience
As summer, satin, nightingale or rose,
Of the senses making sense –
Follow my nose,

Attend all other points of contact,
Deserve your berth:
My brain-child, help me find my own way back
To fire, air, water, earth.
I am, in fact,

More than a bag of skin and bone.
My person is
A chamber where the elements postpone
In lively synthesis,
In peace on loan,

Old wars of flood and earthquake, storm
And holocaust,
Their attributes most temperately reformed
Of heatwave and of frost.
They take my form,

Learn from my arteries their pace –
They leave alarms
And excursions for my heart and lungs to face.
I hold them in my arms
And keep in place.

To walk, to run, to leap, to stand –
Of the litany
Of movement I the vicar in command,
The prophet in my country,
The priest at hand,

Take steps to make it understood
The occupants
Assembled here in narrow neighbourhood
Are my constituents
For bad or good.

Body and Mind, I turn to you.
It's me you fit.
Whatever you think, whatever you do,
Include me in on it,
Essential Two.

Who house philosophy and force,
Wed well in me
The elements, for fever's their divorce,
Nightmare and ecstasy,
And death of course.

My sponsor, Mind, my satellite,
Keep my balance,
Steer me through my heyday, through my night,
My senses' common sense,
Selfcentred light.

And you who set me in my ways,
Immaculate,
In full possession of my faculties –
Till you disintegrate,
Exist to please.

Lest I with fears and hopes capsize,
By your own lights
Sail, Body, cargoless towards surprise.
And come, Mind, raise your sights –
Believe my eyes.

## Persephone

### 1

I see as through a skylight in my brain
The mole strew its buildings in the rain,

The swallows turn above their broken homes
And all my acres in delirium.

### 2

Straightjacketed by cold and numskulled
Now sleep the well-adjusted and the skilled –

The bat folds its wing like a winter leaf,
The squirrel in its hollow holds aloof.

### 3

The weasel and ferret, the stoat and fox
Move hand in glove across the equinox.

I can tell how softly their footsteps go –
Their footsteps borrow silence from the snow.

## Elegy for Fats Waller

for Solly Lipsitz

Lighting up, lest all our hearts should **break,**
His fiftieth cigarette of the day,
Happy with so many notes at his beck
And call, he sits there taking it away,
The maker of immaculate slapstick.

With music and with such precise rampage
Across the deserts of the blues a trail
He blazes, towards the one true mirage,
Enormous on a nimble-footed camel
And almost refusing to be his age.

He plays for hours on end and though **there be**
Oases one part water, two parts gin,
He tumbles past to reign, wise and thirsty,
At the still centre of his loud dominion –
THE SHOOK THE SHAKE THE SHEIKH OF
    ARABY.

## In Memoriam

My father, let no similes eclipse
Where crosses like some forest simplified
Sink roots into my mind, the slow sands
Of your history delay till through your eyes
I read you like a book. Before you died,
Re-enlisting with all the broken soldiers
You bent beneath your rucksack, near collapse,
In anecdote rehearsed and summarized
These words I write in memory. Let yours
And other heartbreaks play into my hands.

Now I see in close-up, in my mind's eye,
The cracked and splintered dead for pity's sake
Each dismal evening predecease the sun,
You, looking death and nightmare in the face
With your kilt, harmonica and gun,
Grow older in a flash, but none the wiser
(Who, following the wrong queue at The Palace,
Have joined the London-Scottish by mistake),
Your nineteen years uncertain if and why
Belgium put the kibosh on the Kaiser.

Between the corpses and the soup canteens
You swooned away, watching your future spill.
But, as it was, your proper funeral urn
Had mercifully smashed to smithereens,
To shrapnel shards that sliced your testicle.
That instant I, your most unlikely son,
In No Man's Land was surely left for dead,
Blotted out from your far horizon.
As your voice now is locked inside my head,
I yet was held secure, waiting my turn.

Finally, that lousy war was over.
Stranded in France and in need of proof
You hunted down experimental lovers,
Persuading chorus girls and countesses:
This, father, the last confidence you spoke.
In my twentieth year your old wounds woke
As cancer. Lodging under the same roof
Death was a visitor who hung about,
Strewing the house with pills and bandages,
Till he chose to put your spirit out.

Though they overslept the sequence of events
Which ended with the ambulance outside,
You lingering in the hall, your bowels on fire,
Tears in your eyes, and all your medals spent,
I summon girls who packed at last and went
Underground with you. Their souls again on hire,
Now those lost wives as recreated brides
Take shape before me, materialize.
On the verge of light and happy legend
They lift their skirts like blinds across your eyes.

## Lares

for Raymond Warren

### Farls

Cut with a cross, they are propped
Before the fire: it will take

Mug after mug of stewed tea,
Inches of butter to ease

Christ's sojourn in a broken
Oatmeal farl down your throat.

### Bridget

Her rush cross over the door
Brings Bridget the cowherd home,

Milk to the dandelion,
Bread to the doorstep, the sun's

Reflection under her foot
Like a stone skimmed on water.

### Furrows

My arm supporting your spine
I lay you out beneath me

Until it is your knuckles,
The small bones of foot and hand

Strewing a field where the plough
Swerves and my horses stumble.

### Beds

The livestock in the yard first,
Then the cattle in the field

But especially the bees
Shall watch our eyelids lower,

Petal and sod folding back
To make our beds lazy-beds.

### Neighbours

Your hand in mine as you sleep
Makes my hand a bad neighbour

Who is moving through stable
And byre, or beside the well

Stooping to skim from your milk
The cream, the dew from your fields.

### Patrick

As though it were Christ's ankle
He stoops to soothe in his hand

The stone's underside: whose spine's
That ridge of first potatoes,

Whose face the duckweed spreading
On a perfect reflection.

## *Caravan*

A rickety chimney suggests
The diminutive stove,
Children perhaps, the pots
And pans adding up to love –

So much concentrated under
The low roof, the windows
Shuttered against snow and wind,
That you would be magnified

(If you were there) by the dark,
Wearing it like an apron
And revolving in your hands
As weather in a glass dome,

The blizzard, the day beyond
And – tiny, barely in focus –
Me disappearing out of view
On probably the only horse,

Cantering off to the right
To collect the week's groceries,
Or to be gone for good
Having drawn across my eyes

Like a curtain all that light
And the snow, my history
Stiffening with the tea-towels
Hung outside the door to dry.

# Two Love Poems

## *Swans Mating*

Even now I wish that you had been there
Sitting beside me on the riverbank:
The cob and his pen sailing in rhythm
Until their small heads met and the final
Heraldic moment dissolved in ripples.

This was a marriage and a baptism,
A holding of breath, nearly a drowning,
Wings spread wide for balance where he trod,
Her feathers full of water and her neck
Under the water like a bar of light.

## *Galapagos*

Now you have scattered into islands –
Breasts, belly, knees, the mount of Venus,
Each a Galapagos of the mind
Where you, the perfect stranger, prompter
Of throw-backs, of hold-ups in time,

Embody peculiar animals –
The giant tortoise hesitating,
The shy lemur, the iguana's
Slow gaze in which the *Beagle* anchors
With its homesick scientist on board.

## Badger

for Raymond Piper

### I

Pushing the wedge of his body
Between cromlech and stone circle,
He excavates down mine shafts
And back into the depths of the hill.

His path straight and narrow
And not like the fox's zig-zags,
The arc of the hare who leaves
A silhouette on the sky line.

Night's silence around his shoulders,
His face lit by the moon, he
Manages the earth with his paws,
Returns underground to die.

### 2

An intestine taking in
patches of dog's-mercury,
brambles, the bluebell wood;
a heel revolving acorns;
a head with a price on it
brushing cuckoo-spit, goose-grass;
a name that parishes borrow.

### 3

For the digger, the earth-dog
It is a difficult delivery
Once the tongs take hold,

Vulnerable his pig's snout
That lifted cow-pats for beetles,
Hedgehogs for the soft meat,

His limbs dragging after them
So many stones turned over,
The trees they tilted.

## Casualty

Its decline was gradual,
A sequence of explorations
By other animals, each
Looking for the easiest way in –

A surgical removal of the eyes,
A probing of the orifices,
Bitings down through the skin,
Through tracts where the grasses melt,

And the bad air released
In a ceremonious wounding
So slow that more and more
I wanted to get closer to it.

A candid grin, the bones
Accumulating to a diagram
Except for the polished horns,
The immaculate hooves.

And this no final reduction
For the ribs began to scatter,
The wool to move outward
As though hunger still worked there,

As though something that had followed
Fox and crow was desperate for
A last morsel and was
Other than the wind or rain.

## Letter to James Simmons

*We were distracted by too many things . . .*
*the wine, the jokes, the music, fancy gowns.*
*We were no good as murderers, we were clowns.*

– Who stated with the Irish queer
A preference for girls to beer –
Here's an attempt at telling all,
My confession unilateral:
Not that it matters for my part
Because I have your lines by heart,

Because the poetry you write
Is the flicker of a night-light
Picking out where it is able
Objects on the dressing table,
Glancing through the great indoors
Where love and death debate the chores,

And where, beneath a breast, you see
The blue veins in filigree,
The dust in a glass of water,
In a discarded french letter
The millions acting out their last
Collaborations with the past.

Yes, to entertain your buddies
With such transcendental studies
Rather than harmonize with hams
In yards of penitential psalms
I count among your better turns:
Play your guitar while Derry burns,

Pipe up aboard the sinking ship
Two by two . . . But before the trip
A pause, please, while the hundredth line[1]
Squanders itself in facile rhyme –
A spry exposé of our game
But paradigmatic all the same

Like talking on as the twelfth chime
Ends nineteen hundred and ninety-nine,
The millennium and number:
For never milestones, but the camber
Dictates this journey till we tire
(So much for perning in a gyre!):

True to no 'kindred points', astride
No iridescent arc besides,
Each gives the other's lines a twist
Over supper, dinner, breakfast
To make a sort of Moebius Band[2],
Eternal but quotidian . . .

So, post me some octosyllabics
As redolent of death and sex

[1]. This is the second verse-letter in a sequence of four. It contains the hundredth line of the sequence.

[2]. The Moebius Band or Strip is an example of a non-orientable surface. It can be illustrated by taking a strip of paper several times longer than it is wide and sticking the two ends together after twisting one of them by a half turn. It is one-sided in the sense that an ant could crawl along the whole length of the strip without crossing the bounding edge and find himself at the starting point on 'the other side'.

Or keep this for the rainy days
When, mindful of the final phase,
We diagnose it a relapse,
A metric following the steps

Of an ageing ballroom dancer
(Words a bow-tie round a cancer):
Or a reasonable way to move –
A Moonlight Saunter out to prove
That poetry, a tongue at play
With lip and tooth, is here to stay,

To exercise in metaphor
Our knockings at the basement door,
A ramrod mounted to invade
The vulva, Hades' palisade,
The Gates of Horn and Ivory
Or the Walls of Londonderry.

## *Letter to Derek Mahon*

And did we come into our own
When, minus muse and lexicon,
We traced in August sixty-nine
Our imaginary Peace Line
Around the burnt-out houses of
The Catholics we'd scarcely loved,
Two Sisyphuses come to budge
The sticks and stones of an old grudge,

Two poetic conservatives
In the city of guns and long knives,
Our ears receiving then and there
The stereophonic nightmare
Of the Shankill and the Falls,
Our matches struck on crumbling walls
To light us as we moved at last
Through the back alleys of Belfast?

Why it mattered to have you here
You who journeyed to Inishere
With me, years back, one Easter when
With MacIntyre and the lone Dane
Our footsteps lifted up the larks,
Echoing off those western rocks
And down that darkening arcade
Hung with the failures of our trade,

Will understand. We were tongue-tied
Companions of the island's dead
In the graveyard among the dunes,

Eavesdroppers on conversations
With a Jesus who spoke Irish –
We were strangers in that parish,
Black tea with bacon and cabbage
For our sacraments and pottage,

Dank blankets making up our Lent
Till, islanders ourselves, we bent
Our knees and cut the watery sod
From the lazy-bed where slept a God
We couldn't count among our friends,
Although we'd taken in our hands
Splinters of driftwood nailed and stuck
On the rim of the Atlantic.

That was Good Friday years ago –
How persistent the undertow
Slapped by currachs ferrying stones,
Moonlight glossing the confusions
Of its each bilingual wave – yes,
We would have lingered there for less . . .
Six islanders for a ten-bob note
Rowed us out to the anchored boat.

## Letter to Seamus Heaney

From Carrigskeewaun in Killadoon
I write, although I'll see you soon,
Hoping this fortnight detonates
Your year in the United States,
Offering you by way of welcome
To the sick counties we call home
The mystical point at which I tire
Of Calor gas and a turf fire.

Till we talk again in Belfast
Pleasanter far to leave the past
Across three acres and two brooks
On holiday in a post box
Which dripping fuchsia bells surround,
Its back to the prevailing wind,
And where sanderlings from Iceland
Court the breakers, take my stand,

Disinfecting with a purer air
That small subconscious cottage where
The Irish poet slams his door
On slow-worm, toad and adder:
Beneath these racing skies it is
A tempting stance indeed – *ipsis
Hibernicis hiberniores* –
Except that we know the old stories,

The midden of cracked hurley sticks
Tied to recall the crucifix,
Of broken bones and lost scruples,

The blackened hearth, the blazing gable's
Telltale cinder where we may
Scorch our shins until that day
We sleepwalk through a No Man's Land
Lipreading to an Orange band.

Continually, therefore, we rehearse
Goodbyes to all our characters
And, since both would have it both ways,
On the oily roll of calmer seas
Launch coffin-ship and life-boat,
Body with soul thus kept afloat,
Mind open like a half-door
To the speckled hill, the plovers' shore.

So let it be the lapwing's cry
That lodges in the throat as I
Raise its alarum from the mud,
Seeking for your sake to conclude
Ulster Poet our Union Title[1]
And prolong this sad recital
By leaving careful footprints round
A wind-encircled burial mound.

1. The Act of Union between Ireland and England became
operative in 1801. Positions of privilege granted to those who
acquiesced in this are sometimes called Union Titles.

## Wounds

Here are two pictures from my father's head –
I have kept them like secrets until now:
First, the Ulster Division at the Somme
Going over the top with 'Fuck the Pope!'
'No Surrender!': a boy about to die,
Screaming 'Give 'em one for the Shankill!'
'Wilder than Gurkhas' were my father's words
Of admiration and bewilderment.
Next comes the London-Scottish padre
Resettling kilts with his swagger-stick,
With a stylish backhand and a prayer.
Over a landscape of dead buttocks
My father followed him for fifty years.
At last, a belated casualty,
He said – lead traces flaring till they hurt –
'I am dying for King and Country, slowly.'
I touched his hand, his thin head I touched.

Now, with military honours of a kind,
With his badges, his medals like rainbows,
His spinning compass, I bury beside him
Three teenage soldiers, bellies full of
Bullets and Irish beer, their flies undone.
A packet of Woodbines I throw in,
A lucifer, the Sacred Heart of Jesus
Paralysed as heavy guns put out
The night-light in a nursery for ever;
Also a bus-conductor's uniform –
He collapsed beside his carpet-slippers
Without a murmur, shot through the head

By a shivering boy who wandered in
Before they could turn the television down
Or tidy away the supper dishes.
To the children, to a bewildered wife,
I think 'Sorry Missus' was what he said.

## Confessions of an Irish Ether-drinker

### 1

It freezes the puddles,
Films the tongue, its brief lozenge
Lesions of spittle and bile,
Dispersals of weather –

Icicles, bones in the ditch,
The blue sky splintering,
Water's fontanel
Closed like an eyelid.

### 2

My dialect becomes
Compactings of sea sounds,
The quietest drifts,
Each snowed-under
Cul-de-sac of the brain –
Glaucoma, pins and needles,
Fur on the tongue:

Or the hidden scythe
Probing farther than pain,
Its light buried in my ear,
The seed potatoes
Filling with blood –
Nuggets of darkness,
Silence's ovaries.

## The Island

The one saddle and bit on the island
We set aside for every second Sunday
When the priest rides slowly up from the pier.
Afterwards his boat creaks into the mist.
Or he arrives here nine times out of ten
With the doctor. They will soon be friends.

Visitors are few. A Belgian for instance
Who has told us all about the oven,
Linguists occasionally, and sociologists.
A lapsed Capuchin monk who came to stay
Was first and last to fish the lake for eels.
His carved crucifixes are still on sale.

One ship continues to rust on the rocks.
We stripped it completely of wash-hand basins,
Toilet fitments, its cargo of linoleum
And have set up house in our own fashion.
We can estimate time by the shadow
Of a doorpost inching across the floor.

In the thatch blackbirds rummaging for worms
And our dead submerged beneath the dunes.
We count ourselves historians of sorts
And chronicle all such comings and goings.
We can walk in a day around the island.
We shall reach the horizon and disappear.

## Skara Brae

for Denis and Sheila Smyth

A window into the ground,
The bumpy lawn in section,
An exploded view
Through middens, through lives,

The thatch of grass roots,
The gravelly roof compounding
Periwinkles, small bones,
A calendar of meals,

The thread between sepulchre
And home a broken necklace,
Knuckles, dice scattering
At the warren's core,

Pebbles the tide washes
That conceded for so long
Living room, the hard beds,
The table made of stone.

MICHAEL LONGLEY

## Three Posthumous Pieces

### 1

In lieu of my famous last words or
The doctor's hushed diagnosis
Lifting like a draught from the door
My oracular pages, this
Will have fluttered on to the floor –
The first of my posthumous pieces.

### 2

As a sort of accompaniment
Drafted in different-coloured inks
Through several notebooks, this is meant
To read like a riddle from the Sphinx
And not my will and testament –
No matter what anybody thinks.

### 3

Two minuses become a plus
When, at the very close of play
And with the minimum of fuss,
I shall permit myself to say:
This is my Opus Posthumous –
An inspiration in its way.

# *Alibis*

### I

My botanical studies took me among
Those whom I now consider my ancestors.
I used to appear to them at odd moments –
With buckets of water in the distance, or
At the campfire, my arms full of snowy sticks.
Beech mast, hedgehogs, cresses were my diet,
My medicaments badger grease and dock leaves.
A hard life. Nevertheless, they named after me
A clover that flourished on those distant slopes.
Later I found myself playing saxophone
On the Souza Band's Grand Tour of the World.
Perhaps because so much was happening
I started, in desperation, to keep a diary.
(I have no idea what came over me.)
After that I sat near a sunny window
Waiting for pupils among the music-stands.
At present I am drafting appendices
To lost masterpieces, some of them my own –
Requiems, entertainments for popes and kings.
From time to time I choose to express myself
In this manner, the basic line. Indeed,
My one remaining ambition is to be
The last poet in Europe to find a rhyme.

### 2

I wanted this to be a lengthy meditation
With myself as the central character –

Official guide through the tall pavilions
Or even the saviour of damaged birds.
I accepted my responsibilities
And was managing daily after matins
And before lunch my stint of composition.
But gradually, as though I had planned it,
And with only a few more pages to go
Of my *Apologia Pro Vita Mea*,
There dawned on me this idea of myself
Clambering aboard an express train full of
Honeymoon couples and football supporters.
I had folded my life like a cheque book,
Wrapped my pyjamas around two noggins
To keep, for a while at least, my visions warm.
Tattered and footloose in my final phase
I improvised on the map of the world
And hurtled to join, among the police files,
My obstreperous bigfisted brothers.

3

I could always have kept myself to myself
And, falling asleep with the light still on,
Reached the quiet conclusion that this
(And this is where I came in) was no more than
The accommodation of different weathers,
Whirlwind tours around the scattered islands,
Telephone calls from the guilty suburbs,
From the back of the mind, a simple question
Of being in two places at the one time.

## Options

for Michael Allen

> *Ha! here's three on's are sophisticated.*
> *Thou art the thing itself.*

These were my options: firstly
To have gone on and on –
A garrulous correspondence
Between me, the ideal reader
And – a halo to high-light
My head – that outer circle
Of critical intelligences
Deciphering – though with telling
Lacunae – my life-story,
Holding up to the bright mirrors
Of expensive libraries
My candours in palimpsest,
My collected blotting papers.

Or, at a pinch, I could have
Implied in reduced haiku
A world of suffering, swaddled
In white silence like babies
The rows of words, the mono-
Syllabic titles – my brain sore
And, as I struggled to master
The colon, my poet's tongue
Scorched by nicotine and coffee,
By the voracious acids
Of my *Ars Poetica*,
My clenched fist – towards midnight –
A paperweight on the language.

Or a species of skinny stanza
Might have materialized
In laborious versions
After the Finnish, for epigraph
The wry juxtaposing of
Wise-cracks by Groucho or Mae West
And the hushed hexameters
Of the right pastoral poet
From the Silver Age – Bacchylides
For instance – the breathings reversed,
The accents wrong mostly – proof –
If such were needed – of my humour
Among the big dictionaries.

These were my options, I say –
Night-lights, will-o'-the-wisps
Out of bog-holes and dark corners
Pointing towards the asylum
Where, for a quid of tobacco
Or a snatch of melody,
I might have cut off my head
In so many words – to borrow
A diagnosis of John Clare's –
Siphoning through the ears
Letters of the alphabet
And, with the vowels and consonants,
My life of make-believe.

## *In Memory of Gerard Dillon*[1]

### 1

You walked, all of a sudden, through
The rickety gate which opens
To a scatter of curlews,
An acre of watery light; your grave
A dip in the dunes where sand mislays
The sound of the sea, earth over you
Like a low Irish sky; the sun
An electric light bulb clouded
By the sandy tides, sunlight lost
And found, a message in a bottle.

### 2

You are a room full of self-portraits,
A face that follows us everywhere;
An ear to the ground listening for
Dead brothers in layers; an eye
Taking in the beautiful predators –
Cats on the windowsill, birds of prey
And, between the diminutive fields,
A dragonfly, wings full of light
Where the road narrows to the last farm.

### 3

Christening robes, communion dresses,
The shawls of factory workers,
A blind drawn on the Lower Falls.

1. The Irish painter Gerard Dillon was born in the Lower
Falls district of Belfast in 1916. He died in 1971.

# Two Love Poems

## *The Lodger*

The lodger is writing a novel.
We give him the run of the house
But he occupies my mind as well –
An attic, a lumber-room
For his typewriter, notebooks,
The slowly accumulating pages.

At the end of each four-fingered
Suffering line the angelus rings –
A hundred noons and sunsets
As we lie here whispering,
Careful not to curtail our lives
Or change the names he has given us.

## *Check-up*

Let this be my check-up:
Head and ear on my chest
To number the heart-beats,
Finger-tips or your eyes
Taking in the wrinkles
And folds, and your body

Weighing now my long bones,
In the palm of your hand
My testicles, future:
Because if they had to
The children would eat me –
There's no such place as home.

## Ars Poetica

### 1

Because they are somewhere in the building
I'll get in touch with them, the wife and kids –
Or I'm probably a widower by now,
Divorced and here by choice, on holiday
And paying through the nose for it: a queue
Of one outside the bathroom for ever
And no windows with a view of the sea.

### 2

I am writing a poem at the office desk
Or else I am forging business letters –
What I am really up to, I suspect,
Is seducing the boss's secretary
Among the ashtrays on the boardroom table
Before absconding with the petty cash box
And a one way ticket to Katmandu.

### 3

I go disguised as myself, my own beard
Changed by this multitude of distortions
To stage whiskers, my hair a give-away,
A cheap wig, and my face a mask only –
So that, on entering the hall of mirrors
The judge will at once award the first prize
To me and to all of my characters.

### 4

After I've flown my rickety bi-plane
Under the Arc de Triomphe and before
I perform a double back-somersault
Without the safety net and – if there's time –
Walk the high wire between two waterfalls,
I shall draw a perfect circle free-hand
And risk my life in a final gesture.

### 5

Someone keeps banging the side of my head
Who is well aware that it's his furore,
His fists and feet I most want to describe –
My silence to date neither invitation
Nor complaint, but a stammering attempt
Once and for all to get him down in words
And allow him to push an open door.

### 6

I am on general release now, having
Put myself in the shoes of all husbands,
Dissipated my substance in the parlours
Of an entire generation and annexed
To my territory gardens, allotments
And the desire – even at this late stage –
To go along with the world and his wife.

## *Fleance*

I entered with a torch before me
And cast my shadow on the backcloth
Momentarily: a handful of words,
One bullet with my initials on it –
And that got stuck in a property tree.

I would have caught it between my teeth
Or, a true professional, stood still
While the two poetic murderers
Pinned my silhouette to history
In a shower of accurate daggers.

But as any illusionist might
Unfasten the big sack of darkness,
The ropes and handcuffs, and emerge
Smoking a nonchalant cigarette,
I escaped – only to lose myself.

It took me a lifetime to explore
The dusty warren beneath the stage
With its trapdoor opening on to
All that had happened above my head
Like noises-off or distant weather.

In the empty auditorium I bowed
To one preoccupied caretaker
And, without removing my make-up,
Hurried back to the digs where Banquo
Sat up late with a hole in his head.

## Death-Watch

I keep my own death-watch:
Mine the disembodied eye
At the hole in my head,
That blinks, watches through
Judas-hatch, fontanel:

Thus, round the clock, the last
Rites again and again:
A chipped mug, a tin plate
And no one there but myself,
My own worst enemy.

# MORE ABOUT PENGUINS
## AND PELICANS

*Penguinews*, which appears every month, contains details of all the new books issued by Penguins as they are published. From time to time it is supplemented by *Penguins in Print*, which is a complete list of all titles available. (There are some five thousand of these.)

A specimen copy of *Penguinews* will be sent to you free on request. For a year's issues (including the complete lists) please send 50p if you live in the British Isles, or 75p if you live elsewhere. Just write to Dept EP, Penguin Books Ltd, Harmondsworth, Middlesex, enclosing a cheque or postal order, and your name will be added to the mailing list.

*In the U.S.A.:* For a complete list of books available from Penguin in the United States write to Dept CS, Penguin Books Inc., 7110 Ambassador Road, Baltimore, Maryland 21207.

*In Canada:* For a complete list of books available from Penguin in Canada write to Penguin Books Canada Ltd, 41 Steelcase Road West, Markham, Ontario.

# PENGUIN MODERN POETS

*Not for sale in the U.S.A.

†Not for sale in the U.S.A. or Canada